ESSAYS AND STUDIES
1968

ESSAYS AND STUDIES

1968

BEING VOLUME TWENTY-ONE OF THE NEW SERIES
OF ESSAYS AND STUDIES COLLECTED FOR
THE ENGLISH ASSOCIATION
BY SIMEON POTTER

JOHN MURRAY
FIFTY ALBEMARLE STREET LONDON

© The English Association 1968

Printed in Great Britain by
Cox & Wyman Ltd, London, Fakenham and Reading
SBN 7195 1806 7

Contents

I

Mirth in Manuscripts

ROSSELL HOPE ROBBINS

Whereas, Research in manuscripts is enjoyable, and
Whereas, Middle English studies are hindered by lack of
    research in manuscripts,
Resolved, that students and scholars further Middle English
    studies through research in manuscripts—and enjoy
    themselves.

IN the twentieth century mirth has several meanings; similarly in the fourteenth. Of the *OED*'s fourth major definition, 'merriment, hilarity,' one would not expect examples in ME manuscripts. For that matter, not much hilarity occurs in ME literature: of several thousand poems, from *Dame Sirith* to *The Freiris of Berwick*, for example, but twenty or thirty could classify as 'merry tales'.[1] The rare instances of manuscript merriment result from the unexpected scribal aside, like the delicious *cri de coeur* of some child, 'ffor pater noster and for my cryde I was full sore I-byte, but I was natt byte I-now',[2] or the bristling annotations against some anti-feminine stanzas in a *Fall of Princes*: 'Ye will be shent' or 'Be pees or I wil redde this leef out of your booke'.[3]

The 'mirth' I wish to advocate in this essay is the *OED*'s first definition of 'pleasurable feeling, enjoyment, gratification'. Such

---

[1] Cf. J. S. P. Tatlock, 'Medieval Laughter', *Speculum*, XXI (1946), 289–94; Beatrice White, 'Medieval Mirth', *Anglia*, LXXVIII (1960), 284–301.

[2] Harley 218, f. 52r. It might also be a copybook exercise; cf. William Nelson, *A Fifteenth Century School Book* (Oxford, 1956), p. 33, No. 137: 'The rules that I must say to my maister ar scantly halfe writyn, wherefore I am worthy to be beet.'

[3] Eleanor Prescott Hammond, 'Two British Museum Manuscripts', *Anglia*, XXVIII (1905), 20.

mirth was happily glossed by drama critic Eric Bentley in a recent *Columbia University Forum*:[4]

> Aristotle has it that learning is a pleasure. . . . Elementary arithmetic provides little spurts of pleasure, as the infant mind receives the sensation of mastery: if it doesn't, then arithmetic is not learned. Now, if feeling plays an integral part in learning at such an elementary level, instead of being eliminated at the more advanced level it plays a progressively greater part all the time, and the advanced student in any field is the supreme hedonist, which is the basis for Shaw's remark to the effect that Isaac Newton must have got a lot more fun out of life than Casanova.

I have got a lot of fun out of life. From personal knowledge, I think the researcher in manuscripts experiences very intensely this kind of mirth. Such is my conviction; it cannot be proved, it can only be shared.

The usual reason for looking at a manuscript is simply to find a text. But the researcher inevitably passes beyond the primary interest in the words to secondary interests that encompass the complete range of man's activities. Alongside the text he is transcribing will be a related or even tangential piece that reveals new insights on life and letters in the Middle Ages. To read a manuscript is a liberal education. In addition, the manuscript researcher may enjoy the excitement of first-time discoveries, no less gratifying though minor. No doubt such browsing underpinned Wright and Halliwell's wonderful grab-bag of ME tidbits, the *Reliquiae Antiquae*.[5] From similar venerable remains a researcher, with a few years' experience, can construct his own reliquary. Here are a few of my relics, all unpublished; I hope there is a bijou to share with everyone.

For the folklorist desirous of filling in the 'T' section of his motif-index, a curious myth about nuns: 'Wommen of religion

[4] Eric Bentley, 'Vietnam: The State of Our Feelings', *Columbia University Forum*, X (1967), 9.

[5] Thomas Wright and James O. Halliwell, *Reliquiae Antiquae* (London, 1841, 1843).

purge noght, be-cause of rysyng o nyght and synggyng and occupacyon in her seruyse her blod wastyth.' And an equally curious frequency myth, somewhat diminished in scientific value by absence of an age factor, in a Middle English *Doctrina et Consilium Galiensis*: 'Thryes a wook, þat is to seyne, If so beo þat of þy manly raysoun þowe feel þyself of so noble and strong corage with-oute þ'enpeyryng of þy persone, þanne thryes a wooke pay þy dette which þowe art bounden to by þe bonde of þy mariage.'[6] The insertion of a section on 'lecherye in spowsebreche' into a variant translation of *Somme le Roi* is unfortunately not an English medieval ploy to guarantee harmony in a disrupted household, but a translation from the Old Testament (Numbers v). It is, however, not explicitly presented as a Biblical ordeal save in a rubric, '*Lex zelotopie*'. To test a wife's fidelity:[7]

The preest shall make hyre before god to stonde, and gyffe hyre in hire handes a dysshe of holyed watyr in a vessell of glasse. And the preest shall take of the erthe that lyeth on the payment [*pavement*] of the tempulle and shall do in the vessell that she holdith in hyre hondes, and she shall make nakyd her hede. And she shall holde the sacryfyce aboue hyre hed, And she shall curse the watyr that she holdith in hyre hondes.

The priest then writes the 'malysons and cursynges' on a piece of parchment and puts it in the vessel so that the ink comes off. Then, having sworn her innocence on pain of becoming crippled, the woman drinks the water. 'And yf she be gylty of the synne that hyr lord by hyr sayde, hyre wombe shall bolne [*swell*] and hyre hippe roote [*rot*]. And so she shall be ataynte of hyre spowsebreche. And yf she not gylty were, hit sholde not harme.'
Interested in domestic science or 'home-making'? Would you care to essay medieval lace-making? There is quite a raft of

[6] Egerton 827, f. 25r, and cf. Harley 78, f. 80r.

[7] BM Addit. 30944, ff. 105v–106r. This is a translation of Friar Lorens d'Orleans' *La somme des vices et des vertus*, but is not included in the edition of W. Nelson Francis, based on eight MSS., for *The Book of Vices and Virtues*, EETS 217. 44–6.

patterns 'for þe maner of laces makyng'.[8] You can plan your own Bunratty Castle medieval banquet with authentic dishes,[9] in one manuscript enjoying the little sketches of rabbits, hens, and pigs as you follow the instructions,[10] or you can savour the appetizing recipes in a medieval illuminated Mrs. Beeton or Fanny Farmer,[11] or pore over a little treatise on early-fourteenth-century cookery in the Friar Herebert manuscript.[12] A manuscript in the National Library of Wales will give you not merely cooking recipes, but instructions on carving, with the obligatory technical vocabulary: 'mynce that plouere, disfigur that pecok, sauce that capon, vnlace that cony.'[13]

Or is your bent to early science—or pseudo-science? How about studying a little tract on physiognomy?[14] Could these writings have influenced the rhetorical catalogues of feminine beauty? Here is a description of the grown-up young lady in a '*Destinarea*' in a Durham University manuscript:[15]

> A mayd þat ys borne in þat same syn [*Aries*] shal haue a syn in þe forhed or in þe neke. She shal haue a feyre chere and browes of heuy coloure, rownd lyppys and glessye, a feyre nose and red coloure, and she shal be bysy to loue hyr hosband—and ȝyt þer shal be anger betwyn them.

Have you ever handled a manuscript over twenty feet long by nearly three feet wide? Fitzwilliam Museum has a roll this size: Ripley's Emblematical Scroll, which tells how to prepare the

---

[8] Harley 2320, ff. 52r–70v; two patterns in Arundel 276, f. 8r.

[9] Camb. Univ. Ll. 1. 18; Arundel 344, ff. 134; Royal 8. B. iv, f. 72v.

[10] Harley 1735, ff. 16v–28v; illustrations on ff. 18r, 18v, 19r.

[11] Bodl. SC 21629, Douce 55, very neatly written, approx. 5 by 7 inches.

[12] BM Addit. 46919, ff. 19r–24v.

[13] NLW Peniarth 394, pp. 93.

[14] Cotton Vesp. E. xvi, ff. 83r–85r, beg. 'Among all þinges who þat woll knowe the mervelous science of ffysnomy he shall knowe the nature and condicion of all folke.'

[15] Durham Univ. Cosin V. v. 13, f. 1r; cf. D. S. Brewer, 'The Ideal of Feminine Beauty in Medieval Literature', *MLR*, L (1955), 257–69.

Philosopher's Stone, with lavish illustrations.[16] The other seven known texts are all rolls, but none so big as this;[17] two Ashmole rolls are several yards long, however.[18] These are the so-called 'hocus-pocus' rolls, designed to be displayed in an alchemist's shop to impress his customers. They were no doubt produced in bulk, commercially, for one other similar roll is apparently unfinished;[19] it has the drawings but lacks the text. The text is similar to the verses quoted from 'Arnold of the Newe Toun' at the end of Chaucer's Canon's Yeoman's Tale.[20]

A student of religion may have wondered how much a votive mass might cost. Thomas Urston, chaplain at Lyme in Cheshire, *ca.* 1477–89, has left a narrow slip of paper, about seven inches by three-quarters, on which he recorded his fees:[21]

These bene the ratys þat I haue hade syn I come to Mersay: ffor iiij dyrgees xiiij d and ... pens, v d; pro missis, vi d, xxi d, xix d. Item: i dirge, iii d. Item: iii dirges, x d. Item: for saying mas ii days at longens, iv d. Item: a dirge, iiij d, xij d. Item: iii dirgis, viij d.

A gamesman may wish to know diversions for a rainy afternoon. A Bodleian manuscript will teach him various methods of secret writing (by using consonants for vowels, etc.), how to make it appear that maggots are crawling on meat by using pieces of catgut, how to guess what sum of money a person thinks of, and how to make an apple move on a table by means of a beetle.[22]

A few other offerings:

To local historians, a manuscript, compiled in the reign of Henry VIII, with several large plans of towns, castles, fortifications

[16] Fitzwilliam Mus. 276*.

[17] No. 1364.5 in Rossell Hope Robbins and John L. Cutler, *Supplement to the Index of Middle English Verse* (Lexington, Kentucky, 1965).

[18] Bodl. SC 7662, Ashmole Rolls 52 and Bodl. SC 8447, Ashmole Rolls 40.

[19] Bodl. SC 8447, Ashmole Rolls 54.

[20] *CT*, G. 1431–46.

[21] Bodl. SC 1980, Bodley 123, f. 51v.

[22] Bodl. SC 21831, Douce 257, ff. 71r, 79r, 80r, 82v.

(especially notable are those for Kingston-upon-Hull, i.e. Hull),[23] or a roll with some very good drawings of London and Colchester in 1485.[24]

To drama historians, some overlooked pageants on the occasion of the visitations of Henry VII to provincial towns,[25] and of Prince Arthur's marriage to Princess Katharine in 1501,[26] and two pageant addresses.[27]

To armchair travellers, a series of aids to augment Mandeville, Marco Polo, and Wey:[28] a couple of guides to Jerusalem, one including the shrines with appropriate Latin prayers, and a caution that 'itt is bihovable to euery cristian to that viage purposing, first to haue his license of oure hooli fader the pope';[29] two prose notes on remarkable things to do and see on the pilgrimage;[30] a late-fifteenth-century itinerary, 'The Way to Rome thorow France';[31] and a collection of French and English phrases for the use of travellers.[32]

To vignerons, a list of English names of wines.[33]

To frustrated males, instructions how 'to make a woman daunce naked': ' Write thes name in a volume of pur parchment with the blode of an owle also mole vita vasta anima, and put it vnder the

[23] Cotton August. Suppl. 1.

[24] Bodl. SC 2986, Bodley Rolls 5.

[25] Cotton Julius B. xii, ff. 10v–20v.

[26] Cotton Vitell. A. xvi, ff. 182r–195r.

[27] No. 3807 in Carleton Brown and Rossell Hope Robbins, *The Index of Middle English Verse* (New York, 1943) and *Supplement*, No. 1547. 5.

[28] *The Itineraries of William Wey*, ed. G. Williams, Roxburghe Club, No. 76 (1857) (and see *Russell's Boke of Norture*, Roxburghe Club, No. 88 (1867) for map); cf. *Information for Pilgrims Unto the Holy Land*, Roxburghe Club, No. 38, 1824. A memo for travellers to the East, in Cotton App. viii, f. 108v, noted by H. S. Bennett, 'Science and Information in English Writings in the Fifteenth Century,' *RES*, XXXIX (1944), 6, has been printed in *Englische Studien*, VII, 277–84.

[29] Queen's Coll. Oxf. 357; Harley 2333. Fr. W. M. Jacobs (Leyden) is preparing an edition of Harley.

[30] Bodl. SC 1414, Laud Misc. 622, ff. 64v–65v; Bodl. SC 9822, Tanner 2, ff. 139, 140.

[31] Bodl. SC 2067, Bodley 487, f. 73r.

[32] Camb. Univ. Ii. 6. 17; ed. Sturzinger, *Orthog. Gallica*, p. xv.

[33] Bodl. SC 1797, Digby 196, f. 161r. For prices (in 1456) cf. Harley 5396.

threshould of þe dore or of þe house wher she is, and she shall bot in a whill daunce naked and take it away.'[34]

To musicians, some unpublished fifteenth-century songs: a monodic carol, not included in Stevens' *Mediaeval Carols*,[35] a monodic moral song,[36] and two polyphonic songs, on a detached bifolium, similar in appearance and style to those in the well-known Arch. Selden B. 26.[37] Also an early-sixteenth-century song in three parts:[38]

> The sight which ferst my hart dyd strayne,
>   When þat your servaunt I became,
> doth bynd me still for to remayne
>   alweys your owin as now I am;
> And yf ye fynd þat I do fayne,
>   by Iust Iugement my silfe I dam
> to have disdayn, to have disdayne.

Or an English fragment written under three lines of music:[39]

> In willdernys
> þer fond I bes,
>   secret, a-lone,
> in gret distresse,
> remediles,
>   makyng her mone.

To political historians trying to identify emblematic animals in the Galfridian prophecies (which gave Henry VIII and Elizabeth I so much trouble that proclaiming them was made a felony),[40] a

[34] Bodl. SC 7798, Ashmole 1378, p. 73.

[35] Lincoln Coll. Oxf. Lat. D. 89, f. 27v; Index, No. 2053; John Stevens, *Mediaeval Carols* (London, 1952), pp. 12, 100, prints music for two other settings of this same carol.

[36] Hunterian 83, f. 21r; *Index*, No. 2376.

[37] BM Dep. Portland 29,333; *Supplement*, Nos, 270, 317. 5.

[38] Corpus Christi Coll. Oxf. 4, f. iv; *Supplement*, No. 3461.8.

[39] Egerton 3002, f. 2v; *Supplement*, No. 1589.5.

[40] Rupert Taylor, *The Political Prophecy in England*, New York, 1911, pp. 105–7.

couple of cogs, cribs, or ponies: 'the names of the lordeschipis with the bages that perteynyth to the Duke of Yorke',[41] and a key to English and European signs.[42]

To mathematicians, one of several little tracts on 'augrym' or computing with Arabic numerals,[43] or, for recreation, a ME mathematics puzzle.[44]

Even in medicine, a discipline somewhat remote from literature, the manuscript researcher will find documents which illuminate poetry, like the volvelles which illustrate Chaucer's doctor of physic's use of astrology. These volvelles, revolving rota of several vellum discs with a revolving pointer, show the days of the month, signs of the zodiac, symbols of the twelve months, and the days of the lunar and solar year. By knowing the patient's nativity, the day of the onset of the sickness, and the day of treatment, a doctor could calculate from this device the best time to effect a cure.[45] A lovely little example of such a manuscript is Egerton 848, which, though worn and rubbed, still has its original wrap-around black leather binding intact.[46] Ashmole MS. 210 is another doctor's pocket book with volvelle, astrological tables, many coloured drawings, as well as a ME poem on the humours and phlebotomy.[47] Other similar manuscripts lack a volvelle but have prognosticatory

[41] Bodl. SC 1683, Digby 82, f. 1v. A shortened list of the signs of Ricardus Ebor Comes Marche occurs in Bodl. SC 1787, Digby 186, f. 14r. A more general list in Bodl. SC 13814, Rawl. D. 1062, ff. 96v–97r. For poems using the signs see Rossell Hope Robbins, *Historical Poems of the XIVth and XVth Centuries* (New York, 1959), p. 363.

[42] Landsdowne 762, f. 52r; *Supplement*, No. 3412.3.

[43] Bodl. SC 2653, Bodley 790, Item G; Egerton 845; Egerton 2662, ff. 136r–165; and see D. E. Smith, 'An Ancient English Algorism', Teachers College, Columbia Univ., Dept. Maths: *Courses for the Training of Teachers 1909–1910*, pp. 11–19 (repr. ff. 136, 137r); also cf. R. Steele, *EETS* es cxviii. 3–22.

[44] Cotton Vesp. E. vii, f. 135r.

[45] For a detailed account of 'A Mediaeval Physician's Vade Mecum', see C. H. Talbot, *Journal of the History of Medicine and Allied Sciences*, XVI (1961), 213–33.

[46] Egerton 848, approx 5 inches square; rota on f. 22r.

[47] Bodl. SC 6678, Ashmole 210. Another good volvelle, with seven discs, in Trinity Coll. Camb. 1199, f. 122r.

tables,[48] and are designed for carrying on the person, including one manuscript which is so folded that it opens and closes like a concertina.[49]

No doubt all interests can join in the topic made respectable by *Playboy*. A Bodleian manuscript, very neatly written for William Corun, Steward (1461–85) to the Bishop of Winchester, contains 'the ordinaunces and constitucions' governing the Stews in Southwark.[50] They are designed to protect both buyer and seller. If one of the latter is 'kept there ayenst her wille', she is to be encouraged to depart 'and neuer come there no more'. She is to pay her rent to the 'stew holder' (fourteen pence a week), 'but at alle tymes [she] shall haue fre licence and liberte without any interrupcion'. On the other hand, she must not 'drawe any man by his gowne or bi his hod', but let him choose where he will, on pain of a fine of twenty shillings. She must not offer herself, without risking a similar penalty, if she 'hath any sikenes of brennynge'.[51] Perhaps the most curious regulation is a sort of money-back guaranty to the client if he experiences unprofessional conduct: 'Item: if any woman take any monee to lye with any man, but she ly stille with hym til it be þe morwe tyme and þanne arise, she shal make a fyn of vj s. viij d.'

The miscellaneous texts, curiosa or trivia, by-products of literary research, enliven the literary quest and are of inestimable value to scholars in related disciplines, and explain the continued usefulness of gallimaufries like the *Reliquiae Antiquae*, the more historically-oriented *Memorials of London and London Life*,[52] or the many-volumed *Harleian Miscellany*.[53]

If manuscript research provides the satisfaction of transcribing and collecting literary texts and the collateral excitement of

[48] E.g., Bodl. SC 15409, Rawl. D. 939; Harley 937; Lansdowne 331.

[49] Egerton 2724 contains many coloured sketches of the occupations of the months.

[50] Bodl. SC 3737, E. Mus. 229; mentioned in *Bulletin of the History of Medicine*, VII (1939). Cf. Harley 293, f. 68r.

[51] The stews were closed in 1506 and 1546 because of syphilis.

[52] Henry Thomas Riley, *Memorials of London and London Life* (London, 1868).

[53] *The Harleian Miscellany*, various eds., e.g. London, 1808, 9 vols.

revealing the life and thought of the people who wrote and read them, why is it that so few scholars and students pursue such research today? It is because they believe that all work on manuscripts has been done.

They may get this impression from undergraduate courses in ME, which come in pre-packaged texts, in bite-size pieces or selections. Where a manuscript location is appended, it has no more relevance than the printer's name on a well-advertised label. Reading the antiseptic texts of a few lyrics from Harley MS. 2253 will scarcely evoke speculation about their origin and preservation; if it does, Ker's facsimile edition will demonstrate that all the problems have been taken care of by the experts.[54]

In the good old days there was some point in looking at manuscripts. In 1864, when the Early English Text Society was founded, you couldn't get a text even of *Sir Gawain and the Green Knight*.[55] Any manuscript you opened was worth printing. You could spend a 'spare half-hour at the Museum', wrote Furnivall, or have a friend copy a text 'with much good will', and come up with a new book.[56] In the first five years of the EETS, Furnivall produced eight of the forty volumes. Yet within a dozen years, by 1875, the directors were making the same complaint as today's young researcher: 'Interesting unedited MSS. of Romance and Adventure, of social Life, and Fun, are rare indeed, and grow rarer year by year.'[57]

But 'rare' is relative, and fifty years later there were still lots of manuscripts queueing up for publication. In 1920, for example, the *South English Legendary*, the *Northern Homily Collection*, or the *Seven Sages* had not been printed.

In 1968, however, as the student's eyes range over the 260 brown- and blue-clad volumes of the EETS, it must seem hard to

[54] *Facsimile of British Museum MS. Harley 2253*, intro. N. R. Ker, EETS 255 (London, 1965). For a discussion of the problems see my review article of Theo Stemmler, *Die englischen Liebesgedichte des MS. Harley 2253*, in *Anglia*, LXXXII (1964), 505–13.
[55] This was the second volume of the *EETS*. It had previously been published in a limited ed. by Madden for the *Bannatyne Club* in 1839.
[56] Frederick J. Furnivall, *Political, Religious, and Love Poems*, EETS 15 (1866), ix, x.
[57] Untitled report, p. 14, bound in with *EETS* 61.

believe that opportunities for search and research in ME manuscripts still exist.

Nevertheless, with the optimism of the punter hoping for a double in the Irish sweepstakes, a scholar dreams always of making The Great Discovery. Finds have occurred even within the last few decades.

One of the most notable of recent discoveries was *The Book of Margery Kempe*—the first biography, the first book by a woman, the first extended travel book, the first psychological case history in English. *The Times Literary Supplement* in 1934, commenting on its identification (by an extract of de Worde's), speculated that 'there is no knowing what treasures may not yet be found in private libraries and muniment rooms which have existed for centuries undisturbed by the auctioneer or the bonfire'. This manuscript was actually neither lost nor discovered; its owner, Colonel W. Bowden-Bowden, wrote:[58]

The manuscript has lain in a bookshelf in the library of Pleasington Old Hall, Lancashire, next to a missal of 1340 in the rite of York, ever since I can remember. We used to look at it occasionally and sometimes visitors read a page or two of it.

The manuscript of Malory was another major discovery, coincidentally in the same year 1934, by an assistant master at Winchester School. Mr. Oakeshott, interested in early bindings, had been allowed to look at the school's medieval manuscripts, then housed in a safe in the Warden's bedroom. Unaware at first of the significance of his find, Oakeshott read in the *Cambridge History of English Literature* the exciting sentence: 'No manuscript of the work is known, and though Caxton certainly revised it, exactly to what extent has never been settled.' 'This sentence,' said Oakeshott, 'made my heart miss a beat.'[59] The manuscript had been

[58] First published in a modern edition by W. Bowden-Bowden (London, 1936). His statement appeared in an article in the *Sunday Observer* (autumn, 1936).

[59] W. F. Oakeshott, 'The Finding of the Manuscript', in *Essays on Malory*, ed. J. A. W. Bennett (Oxford, 1963), p. 3.

overlooked, he supposed, because it was defective and Malory's name had been omitted from the catalogue—and no one had bothered to check it: 'The moral seems to be that there are chances for the humblest gleaner even when the harvest has been reaped by experienced hands.'[60]

Discoveries are not limited to the exclusive private library. In 1960, the very important Blage MS. at Trinity College, Dublin, was found by Professor Kenneth Muir to contain twenty previously unknown poems by Wyatt.[61] In the inadequate catalogue of 1906, the manuscript is stated to contain 'Devotional Poems by G. B. and others'. Medievalists, in fact, had previously examined the first (fifteenth-century) part of the manuscript, but had never troubled about the two further (mid-sixteenth-century) volumes. About 1945 the British Museum acquired a major collection of English and Latin carols with music; Egerton MS. 3303 was readily available to any scholar, and half a dozen worked on it and wrote about it.[62]

In my own thirty-five years of examining manuscripts, I have discovered many ME poems: some minor and dull, like the Epitaph for Duke Humphrey,[63] though valuable for suggesting the use of memorial scrolls in the burial area, antedating Claudio's 'bills' in *Much Ado About Nothing* (V. iii); others minor and charming, like two short love poems, 'Thoythis fre þat lykis me',[64] and 'O ye prynces þat prechyd hase my hert';[65] others minor and amusing, like the little amatory riddle—if the solution be not apparent, it may be found in my article:[66]

[60] Ibid., p. 6.

[61] Blage MS. in Trinity Coll. Dublin, MS. 160 (D. 2. 7); Wyatt poems announced by Muir in *TLS*, 20 March 1960; *London Magazine*, VII, No. 3 (March, 1961), pp. 11–17; *N & O*, n. s. VII (Oct. 1960), 368–70; edited in *Unpublished Poems* (Liverpool, 1961).

[62] For description and bibliography see Richard Leighton Greene, *A Selection of English Carols* (Oxford, 1962), pp. 170–1.

[63] *Neuphilologische Mitteilungen*, LVI (1955), 241–9.

[64] 'A Late Fifteenth-century Love Lyric', *MLN*, LXIX (1954), 153–60.

[65] 'An Unkind Mistress', *MLN*, LXIX (1954), 552–8.

[66] 'Isabel: A Riddling Mistress', *English Language Notes*, I (1963), 1–4.

Chyldern profytt and lycor faylyng—
So hyght my trew loue withowten lesying.
Among spyces my trew loue ys,
Namyd trewly withowtyn myse.
Gardeyn wayes and comfort of floweres—
So hyght my trew loue. how hyght yowres?
Watere frosyn and caym is brothere—
So hyght my trew loue and non othere.

Other discoveries of mine have included major series of ME secular poems, the Findern Anthology[67] and the Newton holograph[68] (two of the three major collections extant), religious collections in privately-owned manuscripts like the Gurney[69] and Delamere,[70] and very recently a long poem on Ugolino, incorporating many lines from Chaucer's Monk's Tale.[71]

Yet the 'humblest gleaner' has as good a chance as the experienced professors (most of whom had overlooked the Blage MS.), if he keeps his eyes open. One could glance through periodicals over recent years and see how a few research students have found manuscript items worthy of publication.[72] And new items can still be flushed out.

[67] *PMLA*, LXIX (1954), 610–42.

[68] 'The Poems of Humfrey Newton, Esquire, 1466–1536', *PMLA*, LXV (1950), 249–81.

[69] 'The Gurney Series of Religious Lyrics', *PMLA*, LIV (1939), 369–90.

[70] 'Speculum Misericordie', *PMLA*, LIV (1939), 935–66.

[71] 'A New Chaucer Analogue: The Legend of Ugolino', *Trivium*, II (1967), 1–16.

[72] I do not know if the following authors were still research students at the time or not, but when they published these articles, they were still junior scholars, and for some of them this was their first article. Now, of course, they have become 'experienced hands', and are my good friends and colleagues: Rachel Corner, 'More Fifteenth-Century Terms of Association', *RES*, n.s. XIII (1962), 229–44; R. J. Frankis, 'Some Late ME Lyrics in the Bodleian Library', *Anglia*, LXXIII (1956), 299–304; A. G. Rigg, 'Some Notes on Trinity College, Cambridge, MS. o. 9. 38', *N&Q*, 211 (1966), 324–30; Celia Sisam, 'Notes on ME Texts', *RES*, n.s. XIII (1962), 385–90; Kenneth Wilson, 'Five Unpublished Secular Love Poems from Trinity College Cambridge MS 599', *Anglia*, LXXIII (1956), 400–18.

Until recently, ME manuscript research concentrated on verse. In editing ME poems, a major difficulty was not knowing the available manuscripts. Furnivall had complained of 'the time that it takes to ascertain whether a poem has been printed or not, which is the best MS. of it, in what points the versions differ, etc. etc.' His solution was to turn himself into 'a foolometer and book-possessor-ometer for the majority of his fellow-[scholars], and print whatever he either does not know, or cannot get at easily'.[73] Proceeding so hurriedly, however, often raised a practical difficulty: 'what was to be done with the already-in-type poor text' when later 'a good text and right arrangement of the poem' was turned up?

Even the most experienced could not be expected to know all the manuscripts of any poem, and editors had to work in a hit or miss fashion until 1920. It takes a lifetime to examine manuscript after manuscript in library after library throughout the world—London, Chicago, Naples, Stockholm, Melbourne, Austin, East Berlin, Aberdeen, New York, Dublin, Paris. Carleton Brown, later General Secretary of the Modern Language Association of America, addressed himself to this lifetime task; in 1916 he published his handlist of manuscripts of ME religious verse, and in 1920 a first-line index of ME religious and didactic poems,[74] listing the manuscripts and editions (where published). It was now possible for an editor of, say, *The Southern Passion* (issued by the EETS in 1933) to know that there were twelve manuscripts, without having to spend years in preliminary research. Brown's *Register* formed the basis of our combined *Index of Middle English Verse*, published in 1943, which added further religious texts as well as secular, trivial, historical, and political poems, increasing the 1920 count of 2,273 entries in 1,100 manuscripts to 4,365 entries in over 2,000 manuscripts. It was now possible, with 41 manuscripts listed, to prepare an edition of Lydgate's *Life of Our Lady*.[75] In the past twenty-one years I have continued combing the libraries,

[73] Furnivall, *EETS* 15 (1866), ix, xviii.

[74] Carleton Brown, *A Register of ME Religious and Didactic Verse* (Oxford, 1916, 1920).

[75] Joseph A. Lauritis, Ralph A. Klinefelter, and Vernon F. Gallagher, *A Critical Edition of John Lydgate's Life of Our Lady* (Pittsburgh, 1961).

and in 1965, with the help of Professor John L. Cutler, published the *Supplement*, which amplifies 2,000 of the former entries and adds 1,500 further entries. It is now possible, with 116 known manuscripts, for some scholar or team to edit *The Pricke of Conscience*—printed only once, in 1863 in Berlin, in a limited edition.[76] From time to time it is probable that a new poem will crop up—one or two since 1965 have already appeared;[77] but for all practical purposes, the entire domain of ME verse has been exhaustively surveyed.

While research in ME verse is still possible and desirable, there exist far more opportunities for original search and research in ME prose.

This is not the first time attention has been directed to the wealth of ME prose, and H. S. Bennett in 1944 pointed to well over fifty works needing modern editions.[78] Discussing ME medical texts, for example, and limiting himself to the Sloane collection only, Bennett gave a figure of 40 unedited manuscripts; had he added medical herbals and plague tractates he could have raised his figure to almost 70. 'Of documents', he observed, 'the increase in the use of English is so rapid and so widespread [in the fifteenth century] that it would be a well-nigh impossible task to list the vernacular output.'[79]

No one who hasn't spent considerable time examining manuscripts has any idea of the wealth of ME prose texts—in all areas: medicine and history and sermons and science and alchemy and travel and religious literature. ME prose is now the only area left in all English literature where a scholar, novice or expert, can

[76] Richard Morris, Philogical Society, Berlin, 1863, from Cotton Galba E. ix.

[77] Three new texts listed by Roger Lass from Yale Univ. 163, *Anglia*, LXXXIII (1965), 172–5; two tags from Merton Coll. Oxf. 248, pr. *Early ME Verse and Prose*, ed. J. A. W. Bennett and G. V. Smithers (Oxford, 1966), p. 128; a description of Rome in PRO, SC 6/956/5, pr. V. J. Scattergood, *Archiv*, CCIII (1967), 279–81; details of the Robartes MS. (now Bodl. Lat. Misc. b. 17) by Saara Nevanlinna, *NM*, LXVII (1966), 56–68; short prayer from Lyell 30, f. 15v, communicated by Douglas Gray.

[78] 'Science and Information in English Writings of the Fifteenth Century', *MLR*, XXXIX (1944), 1–8; see also H. S. Bennett, 'Fifteenth-Century Secular Prose', *RES*, XXI (1945), 257–63.

[79] Bennett, *MLR*, XXXIX. 8.

partake of that fresh spring morning feeling of elation and exuberance that Furnivall and Skeat and Morris said they felt when they were pouring out their new texts in the mid-nineteenth century.

Lest it be thought I am exaggerating the interest this mass of material holds, let me refer to Professor William Matthews, who compiled a very varied sampler of *Later Medieval English Prose* with a reasoned and reasonable estimate of its literary qualities:[80]

> Among the [55] medieval writers who are represented in this volume only a few can be said to be excellent stylists or in any way original, yet to the generous taste by which literature lives few of them can seem dull.

I echo his concluding sentence that ME prose 'is not very well known, and the compiler's hope is that the samplings will give enough pleasure to lead the reader into further explorations and finer discriminations'.

For the immediate present, however, I would emphasize 'further explorations', since for making texts available 'finer discriminations' are not necessary. First we must know what is there. The manuscripts of ME prose today are only slightly less unknown than those of English poetry when the EETS was founded some 260 volumes ago: then as now, an editor of a text could not be certain he had all the manuscripts.

One would expect at least Chaucer's manuscripts to be known. Of the *Astrolabe*, Skeat listed 22 manuscripts, as did Pintelon in his 1940 edition.[81] Robinson added three more manuscripts.[82] However, Robinson was unaware of two other manuscripts of the *Astrolabe*, Sloane 446[83] and Aberdeen University.[84] The EETS edition of *The Book of Vices and Virtues* knew of eight manuscripts; there happens to be a ninth.[85] Hamelius in 1919 based his

[80] New York, 1963, p. 27.

[81] P. Pintelon, *Chaucer's Treatise on the Astrolabe* (Antwerp, 1940).

[82] F. N. Robinson, *The Works of Geoffrey Chaucer* (Boston, 1957), p. 921.

[83] Sloane 446, ff. 50r–56.

[84] Aberdeen Univ. 123, ff. 10v–30r. This MS. was not available when M. R. James compiled his *Catalogue* (Aberdeen, 1932).

[85] BM Addit. 30944, ff. 154.

EETS edition of *Mandeville's Travels* on only four manuscripts; Josephine Bennett in 1954 listed 36 (ME) manuscripts with three untraced manuscripts (excluding the rhymed versions),[86] and M. C. Seymour, who is preparing a new edition for the EETS, listed 36.[87] But he overlooked a sizeable fragment in the Bodleian.[88]

In the quarter of a century since Bennett wrote, few young scholars (despite reports) took the hint; at any rate, no editions of his desiderata have appeared. Because of this neglect, I think it necessary to spell out anew the only conclusion possible from the foregoing paragraphs.

The most urgent of all ME projects, taking precedence over bibliographies and critical studies of published works, is an index of ME prose, comparable to the index for the verse.[89] Until this is done, knowledge will remain episodic and uncertain.[90]

What is to be done?

To develop among the international academic community a consensus that such a project is worthwhile, and that junior scholars be encouraged to undertake manuscript research. And when a scholar has decided on some project, he should make it known in the 'ME Research in Progress' published annually in *Neuphilologische Mitteilungen*.[91]

How can this be done?

[86] Josephine Waters Bennett, *The Rediscovery of Sir John Mandeville* (New York, 1954), pp. 287–98.

[87] M. C. Seymour, 'The English MSS. of Mandeville's Travels', *Edinburgh Bibliographical Society Transactions*, IV (1966), 169–210.

[88] Bodl. Lat. Misc. E. 85, ff. 84r–91. Parts of chapters xxii–iv, corresponding to pp. 85–101 of the Hakluyt Society ed. by C. R. Beazley, 1903.

[89] On several occasions since 1960 I have spoken and written on the desirability of research in ME prose manuscripts; most recently in *Supplement*, p. xxiv.

[90] Even the publication of the comprehensive *Manual of the Writings in ME, 1050–1500*, gen. ed. J. Burke Severs, will not change the situation, for this work is based on printed editions, not on MSS. The first fascicule on the Romances is now available (MLA, New York, 1967).

[91] Annually since 1963, generally in the second quarterly issue. Items for inclusion to be sent directly to me by December 1 each year (Katsbaan Onderheugel, Saugerties, New York 12477).

Preliminary Aids for Manuscript Research

As aids for basic manuscript research, some handlists are needed; their compilation is an elementary hack job, though the makers will thereby gain a thorough grounding in ME resources:

1. Checklist of catalogues of manuscripts.[92]
2. Bibliography of ME prose items already published.
3. Classified handlist of manuscripts containing ME prose already published (from 2, supplemented from books listing ME prose manuscripts).[93] For each manuscript should be listed *every* prose item (and cross-references to *Index* and *Supplement* for verse items), giving foliation, date, title or descriptive title, approximate length, beginning and concluding sentences[94] and sufficient striking lines to help identification, other texts, publication, and (if known) dialect, provenance, authorship.
4. First-line index of ME prose already published (from 3, by items), arranged alphabetically.
5. Index of subjects, titles, and themes of entries in 4.[95]

[92] Numerous MSS. catalogues are unreliable or incomplete, e.g. Ashmole, Oxford colleges (Coxe), Cambridge Univ., Cotton, Harley, Trinity Coll. Dublin. Others are excellent, e.g. Balliol Coll. Oxf. (Mynors), some Cambridge colleges (James), Royal (Warner and Gilson).

[93] For example: Hope Emily Allen, *Writings Ascribed to Richard Rolle* (New York, 1927); Charles Lethridge Kingsford, *English Historical Literature in the Fifteenth Century* (Oxford, 1913); John M. Manly and Edith Rickert, *The Text of the Canterbury Tales* (Chicago, 1940), Vol. I; G. R. Owst. *Preaching in Medieval England* (Cambridge, 1926), and *Literature and Pulpit in Medieval England* (Cambridge, 1933) (use with care); Eleanor Sinclair Rohde, *The Old English Herbals* (London, 1922) (use with caution); Dorothea Waley Singer, *Catalogue of Latin and Vernacular Alchemical Manuscripts* (Brussels, 1928–31), supplemented by Rossell Hope Robbins, 'Alchemical Texts in ME Verse: Corrigenda and Addenda', *Ambix*, XIII (1966), 62–73; Dorothea Waley Singer, 'Survey of Medical Manuscripts in the British Isles Dating from before the Sixteenth Century', *Proc. Royal Soc. Medicine, Section Hist. of Medicine*, XII (1918–19), 96–107.

[94] Since ME MSS. are written in such different sizes of handwriting and presented in such different formats, I see no reason to give the incipits of the second folio. And most ME prose texts are not acephalous.

[95] Motif indexes are needed for anecdotes in sermons, incidents in saints lives. An index for the latter would form an interesting comparison with Gerald Bordman, *Motif-Index of the English Metrical Romances* (FF Com., No. 190) (Helsinki, 1963).

Basic Manuscript Research 1: Handlists of Manuscripts with ME Prose

A young scholar could start with a collection of manuscripts, or some part of a large collection. He should examine the appropriate catalogue and (with help from Aid 3) list the manuscripts needing close inspection—all ME manuscripts mentioned in the catalogue and all 'suspected' manuscripts, like collections of sermons in Latin, French, or English, prayer books irrespective of provenance (for inserted or flyleaf ME prayers), commonplace books, medical collections (including Latin, for ME items not noted in the catalogue). He should look at every manuscript up to 1550 in the entire collection (for possible earlier texts or flyleaf or marginal additions). The result should be a Manuscript Handlist comparable to Aid 3, listing unpublished as well as published materials. A first-line index can follow.

As an illustration of what he might find, let us look at the Arundel collection in the British Museum. Brown's original *Register* listed 17 manuscripts of ME religious verse; the researcher will find that 50 of the 500 Arundel manuscripts contain ME prose and verse. After recording 14 manuscripts with ME, he will reach MS. 158, a leaf of which was used for a British Museum picture postcard; this manuscript contains Rolle's *English Psalter* (noted by Allen);[96] on f. 8 is a short 'Homily upon Patience and Humility', which should be transcribed, since it has not been identified. Arundel MS. 197 is a collection of devotional tracts; 'Active and Contemplative Life' is not Hilton's, but an extract from the Revelations of St. Bridget;[97] a prose prayer to the Sacrament (ff. 47v–48r) should be transcribed, for it will be found to resemble other prayers at the Levation.[98] Arundel MS. 249 is a *vulgaria* which has been partly printed.[99] Arundel MS. 272 is a

[96] Allen, *Writings . . . Rolle*, pp. 172, 197, with over three dozen other MSS.

[97] See W. P. Cummins, *The Revelations of St. Birgitta*, EETS 178. xix; Joyce Bazire and Eric Colledge, *The Chastising of God's Children* (Oxford, 1957), p. 4, fn 4 (Book VII, chapt. 7). Other texts in Camb. Univ. Ii. 6. 40; Pepys 2125.

[98] 'Hayle holi bodi of oure Lorde Jhesu Criste', also in Univ. Coll. Oxf. 123, f. 74r, and Camb. Univ. Ii. 4. 9. f. 95v. For verse Levation prayers see Robbins, *MP*, XL (1942), 131–46.

[99] William Nelson, *A Fifteenth Century School Book* (Oxford, 1956).

late-fifteenth-century commonplace book, which in addition to the printed '*Agnus Castus*' herbal,[100] has three pages (ff. 63r–64r) of miscellaneous medical receipts; these too should be transcribed. Arundel MS. 279 is a slim volume of ME and Latin sermons; the ME sermons (ff. 2r–10r) should be transcribed, for very few ME sermons are in print. Arundel MS. 285 has been printed in full by J. A. W. Bennett.[101] Arundel MS. 286 is another collection of separate ME devotional and mystical treatises, some not identified.[102] And so it goes: Arundel MS. 334 has some gourmet cookery recipes;[103] Arundel MS. 364, like MS. 112, has Love's *Mirror*;[104] Arundel MS. 359 is an early-sixteenth-century manuscript with a fantastic mishmash of ME prose, and a poem, 'The Order of Shooting with the Crossbow'.[105]

The compilation of such handlists over the next ten to twenty years is feasible, and would form the basis for the envisioned omnibus index of ME prose.

Basic Manuscripts Research II: *Editions of ME Prose Manuscripts*

Some scholars, especially those on the continent or in North America unable to spend several years in British libraries, might happily edit a complete manuscript. The range of suitable manuscripts is extensive; sermons and devotional tracts are very desirable. For many subjects, good editions of like material are available, from which the beginning researcher might obtain some

---

[100] Gösta Bordin, *Agnus Castus*, Upsala, 1950; and in other MSS., e.g. Royal 18. A. vi; BM Addit. 4698.

[101] J. A. W. Bennett, *Devotional Pieces in Verse and Prose*, STS 3rd s. XXIII (1955).

[102] Allen, *Writings . . . Rolle*, pp. 357–8.

[103] Pr. Society of Antiquaries: *Collection of Ordinances and Regulations for the Royal Household* (London, 1790), p. 425.

[104] H. S. Bennett, *OHEL*, 1927, p. 180: 'Some of the most beautiful prose of the century.' Margaret Deansley, *MLR*, XV (1920), 353, says it was more popular than any other book in the fifteenth century. See E. Jones, 'A Study of Nicholas Love's Myrror of the Blessed Life of Jesus Christ' (Ph. D. thesis, Univ. of London, 1949).

[105] *Supplement*, No. 4244.5. Cf. G. Markham, *Country Contentments* (London, 1675).

idea of the type of writings involved as well as some idea of the research required.[106]

If a young scholar undertakes to edit a single work, he must remember the caveat about not being sure of the manuscripts. For some major works I suppose it is better to have some texts rather than nothing, and it probably doesn't matter too much whether thirty or forty manuscripts are used to edit John of Burgundy's plague tract,[107] or ten to twenty for the 'Rosemary' herbal, 'compiled at instance of þe Countesse of Henowde'.[108] *Ad hoc* editions would be valuable: for example, *Body of Policy* (Camb. Univ. Kk. 1. 5), *Crafte of Astronomye* (Bodl. SC 1668), Daniel's urinology (Bodl. SC 3617), *Dives et Pauper* (Harley 149), de Guileville (Bodl. SC 1239), *Life of Adam* (Bodl. SC 21589), or Shirley's translation of *Secreta Secretorum* (BM Addit. 5467).

Other researchers might wish to study a type, species, or

---

[106] For example: for Sermons: T. E. Erbe, *Mirk's Festial*, EETS e.s. xcvi; D. M. Grisdale, *Three ME Sermons from the Worcester Chapter MS. F. 10* (Leeds, 1939); Homer G. Pfander, *The Popular Sermon* (New York, 1937); Woodburn O. Ross, *ME Sermons*, EETS 209; for Devotional Treatises: Phyllis Hodgson, *Deonise Hid Diuinite*, EETS 231; C. Horstman, *Yorkshire Writers* (London, 1895, 1896); Fumio Kuriyagawa, *Walter Hilton's Eight Chapters on Perfection* (Tokyo, 1967); Bjorn Wallner, *Hilton's Qui habitat et Bonum est*, Lund St. in English, XXIII (1954); J. van Zutphen, *Richard Lavynham: A Litil Tretys on the Seven Deadly Sins* (Rome, 1956); for Prayer Books: Francis Wormald, 'The Revelation of the Hundred Pater Nosters', *Laudate*, 1963 (Sept.), 1–17; for Medical Receipts: Warren R. Dawson, *A Leechbook* (London, 1934); Fritz Heinrich, *Ein Mittelenglisches Medizinbuch* (Halle, 1896); G. Henslow, *Medical Works of the Fourteenth Century* (London, 1899); Gottfried Müller, *Aus Mittelenglischen Medizintexten* (Leipzig, 1929); Margaret Sinclair Ogden, *The Liber de Diversis Medicinis*, EETS 207; for Commonplace Books: Nita Scudder Baugh, *A Worcestershire Miscellany* (Philadelphia, 1956); Rudolf Brotanek, *Mittelenglische Dichtungen* (Halle, 1940); Mabel Day, *The Wheatley MS.*, EETS 155; Lucy Toulmin Smith, *A Commonplace Book of the Fifteenth Century* (Norwich, 1886).

[107] Cf. David Murray, *John de Burgundia and the Pestilence* (London, 1891); Dorothea Waley Singer, 'Some Plague Tractates', *Proc. Royal Soc. Medicine, Section Hist. of Medicine*, IX (1916), 159–212; Bennett, *MLR* XXXIX. 3, says he has identified over 40 copies. Singer classifies five ME versions; for a metrical version cf. *Index*, No. 1190, ed. R. H. Bowers, Southern Folklore Qr., xx (1956), 118–25.

[108] Cf. Rohde, *Herbal*, p. 178.

subgenre of literature, from a limited number of manuscripts,[109] like prose prayers at the Sacrament, general confes-
sions, some particular saint's life, or charms found in medical
books.

As suitable for editing in their entirety, I would suggest unpublished manuscripts like the following. Where they contain
many short items, or where items occur in many other manuscripts, complete identification might have to wait.

A. *Sermons (Collections)*: Bodl. SC 1053, Laud Misc. 471; SC
1905, Bodley 95 (Sunday Epistles); SC 2628, Bodley 788
(Wycliffite); SC 2688, Bodley 806 (Sunday Gospels); Bodl.
Holkham Misc. 40; New Coll. Oxf. 95; Camb. Univ. Dd. 10.
50; Gg. 5. 31; Camb. Univ. Add. 5338; Trinity Coll. Camb.
322; Harley 2247; 5085; Royal 18. A. xvii; Gloucester Cath.;
Trinity Coll. Dublin 428 (Saint Days); Morgan Lib. 955.

B. *Devotional Tracts*: Bodl. SC 549, Laud Misc. 38 (*Dyalog of
Seynt Anselme and of Oure Lady*); SC 1291, Laud Misc. 517
(*Manere of Good Lyuyng*); SC 2103, Bodley 220 (*Boke of Seynt
Mawte* = Matilda; another copy in Egerton 2006; Latin
original in Trinity Coll. Oxf. 32); SC 2643, Bodley 789
(includes verse); Bodl. Eng. theol. f. 39 (ca. 1400, includes
sermons);[110] Camb. Univ. Dd. 12. 39 (14th cent.); Arundel 286
(includes Rolle and Benjamin); Cotton Titus C. xix (includes
Rolle); Egerton 826 (14th cent. short tracts); Harley 149
(includes *Dives et Pauper*);[111] 211 (Carmelite: includes Lavynham); 953 (includes *Pore Caitiff*); 1197 (includes verse); 1671
(includes *Weye to Paradys*); 1706[112] (includes Rolle; sister MS.
Bodl. SC 21896); 1740 (Passion texts); 2398 (includes *Speculum
Ecclesie*); 4012; 6615 (includes *Chastising of God's Children*);

[109] Several theses are deposited at the Univ. of London Lib., including G. S.
Ivy, 'Trinity Coll. Camb. MSS. with English Verses'; P. W. Jolliffe, 'Penitential
Formulae and Advise in ME Prose'; and Peter Revelle.

[110] Reported diss. 1963–4, E. P. Wilson (Oxford).

[111] Reported diss. 1965–6, Priscilla Barnum (Syracuse).

[112] Harley 1706 described by A I. Doyle, 'Books Connected with the Vere
Family and Barking Abbey', *Essex Arch. Soc. Trans.*, n.s. XXV (1958), 222–43.
This is a superb account of a devotional MS.

Royal 17. C. xviii (includes Hilton); BM Addit. 15216 (Latin and ME, illuminated); 37709 (includes Juliana, Ruysbroeck);[113] Lambeth 432 (includes *Abbey of Holy Ghost*);[114] Illinois Univ. 80.

C. *Prayer Books (Collections)*:[115] Camb. Univ. Ii. 6. 43 (includes meditations); Camb. Univ. Add. 4120 (ME prose and verse); Cotton Titus A. xix (fervid mystical prose); Harley 494 (some Latin); BM Addit. 10596; Lambeth 559 (includes devotions, some Latin).

D. *Grammatical Collections:* Bodl. SC 4065, Hatton 58 (Latin cases); Royal 17. C. xvii (some verse); BM Addit. 37075 (some Latin, with schoolboy scribbling); Trinity Coll. Dublin 430 (ca. 1500, rules for translating ME into Latin).

E. *Collections of Medical Receipts:* Bodl. SC 1630, Digby 29; SC 2062, Bodley 483; SC 2072, Bodley 177; SC 2073, Bodley 178; SC 2074, Bodley 179; SC 7722, Ashmole 1481; SC 7757, Ashmole 1391; SC 7798, Ashmole 1378; SC 8606, Wood empt. 18; SC 8613, Wood empt. 25; SC 21658, Douce 84; SC 29003, Add. A. 106; All Souls Coll. Oxf. 121; Balliol Coll. Oxf. 329; St. John's Coll. Oxf. 76; Camb. Univ. Ee. 1. 13;

[113] Edition in progress from this and other MSS. by A. I. Doyle.

[114] Reported diss. 1965–6, Cornelius Page (Fordham).

[115] Many ME prose prayers are found singly or in small groups, e.g. Bodl. SC. 1851, Bodley 9, f. 93v (to Jesus); 2322, Bodley 423, f. 165r (to BVM); 2376, Bodley 596, f. 31v (general confession); SC 2604, Bodley 850, f. 83r (various); SC 3615, E. Mus. 35, p. 219; SC 4104, Hatton 31, f. 113v (for Levation); SC 15781, Rawl. liturg. f. 3, 128v (Passion); SC 15802, Rawl. liturg. f. 36, f. 63v ('devout prayer'); SC 18340, Gough liturg. 7 (Latin-ME prayer book for Earl of Shrewsbury, ca 1500); Bodl. Don d. 85, f. 126r (25 Joys); Bodl. Lat, liturg. e. 17. f. 50r; Bodl. Lyell 30, f. 18v (at Levation), f. 176r (5 joys); Trinity Coll. Oxf. 86, f. 1r (general confession); Univ. Coll. Oxf. 123, f. 74r (at Elevation); Camb. Univ. Dd. 10. 21, f. 154v (to Precious Heart); Ff. 6. 8, f. 1r (to BVM); Gg. 1. 6, f. 145v (ME tr. *O intemerata*); Gg. 6. 22, f.. 124v (ME tr. *O mater Dei*); Hh. 1. 11, f. 129v (7 Dignitees BVM), f. 134v (7 Joys); Ii. 4. 9, f. 95r (at Elevation); Ii. 6. 39, f. 163v (ME tr. Thomas Aquinas); Peterhouse Coll. Camb. 276, ff. 4 only (to BVM, general confession); Trinity Coll. Camb. 600, p. 372 (at Elevation); Cotton Faustina D. iv, f. 76r (to Guardian Angel); Harley 1025, f. 175r (to Guardian Angel); 1251, f. 182r (to BVM); 2339, f. 1r; 2445, f. 80v (Sorrows BVM); 3810, f. 60r (general confession); 4011, f. 2v (at Elevation); BM Addit. 33381, f. 181v (to Jesus); Trinity Dublin 92, f. 99v (to All Saints); Illinois Univ. 76.

Caius Coll. Camb. 609; Emmanuel Coll. Camb. 69; Pepys 1662; St. John's Coll. Camb. 37, I; Sidney Sussex Coll. Camb. 58; Trinity Coll. Camb. 921; 1039; 1117; Egerton 833; 848; Harley 950; 1600; 2378; 2389; Lansdowne 680; Royal 16. F. ii; 17. A. iii; 17. A. viii; Sloane 100; 140; 147; 357; 374; 405; 468; 634; 706; 783 B; 962; 965; 2457; 2582; 3153; 3449; 3489; BM Addit. 33971; Aberdeen Univ. 258; NLW Peniarth 369; 370; 388; Trinity Coll. Dublin 369; Univ. Coll. London Lat. 12; Uppingham School; Wellcome Hist. Med. Mus. 7; 115; 225; 409; 410; 537.

F. *Commonplace Books:* Bodl. SC 8538, Wood D. 8 (tracts on horses, herbals, plague, prognostics); SC 10234, Tanner 407 (Robert Reynes of Acle, Norfolk); SC 15559, Rawl. D. 1222 (cookery, medicine, charms); Camb. Univ. LI. I. 18 (cookery, hunting, hawking); Trinity Coll. Camb. 1157 (very miscellaneous notebook); Egerton 1995 (chronicles, religious texts, medicine; some Latin and French); Harley 2252 (John Colyn, mercer of London); Sloane 3215 (largely medical); Lambeth 306 (melange of prose and verse); Morgan Lib. 775 (melange, Vegetius).

These lists are merely representative samples of the numerous manuscripts awaiting editors.[116]

In this consideration of mirth in medieval manuscripts, two of the three elements in ME studies have been presented: the manuscripts and the scholar. There is a third. If the young scholar be a research student, his work may have to be approved and accepted by an English department or faculty. Would it be possible—I ask as one *of*, rather than *in*, the academic community—for English research boards to accept a liberal interpretation of what is (for the purposes of advanced degrees) English literature? Some of this manuscript research is cross-disciplined and, if English has inherited the mantle of Greek and Latin for classical concepts (as some of us once believed), an ecumenical approach may not be out of place. And new texts are the bread (if not the bread-and-butter) of the academic world.

[116] Not included are all the MSS. of historical prose and alchemical prose; see Kingsford, *Eng. Hist. Lit.*; Singer, *Cat. Latin-Vernacular Alchemical MSS.*, and Robbins, *Ambix*, XIII.

At the beginning of this essay, I tried to tantalize potential scholars to an awareness of ME manuscripts by displaying a tray of non-literary goodies. As a rhetorical chiasmus, I should like to offer in conclusion a few literary attractions, lyrics no less, to the potential researchers in non-literary manuscripts.

In sermons and homilies the manuscript researcher is often rewarded; for example, he may come across the celebrated quatrain, often printed, occurring in Latin, French, and English texts of Archbishop Edmund Riche's *Speculum Ecclesie*:[117]

> Now goþ sunne under wode,
> me rueþ, marie, þy faire rode;
> now goþ [sunne] under tre,
> me rueþ, marie, þi sone and þe.

Or the secular scrap quoted in the Latin sermons now on deposit at Tübingen University:[118]

> So longe ic haue, lauedi,
> yhoued at þi gate,
> þat mi fot is ifrore, faire lauedi,
> for þi luue faste to þe stake.

In devotional tracts the manuscript researcher may uncover new variations of Rolle's poems, like the three unique songs in '*Ego Dormio*' in a Trinity College Dublin manuscript, not published since 1836;[119] or verses added at the end of the Latin text of Rolle's *De modo vivendi*, 'a glorious garland of viij rosis':[120]

---

[117] Most recently in Bennett-Smithers, *Early ME Verse and Prose*, p. 129. Text here from Bodl. SC 2315, Bodley 46, f. 136v, previously unpublished [v. 3, MS. *sumer*]. *Index* and *Supplement*, No. 2320; in all, 42 MSS.

[118] Berlin Preussische Staatsbibliothek Lat. theol. fol. 249, f. 131r; *Supplement*, No. 3167.3; previously pr. Robbins, 'ME Lyrics: Handlist of New Texts', *Anglia*, LXXXIII (1965), 47.

[119] Trinity Coll. Dublin 155, pp. 11–17; Index, Nos. 1700, 1717, 1743; pr. *British Magazine and Monthly Register*, IX (1836), 501–2; No. 1700 also pr. Carleton Brown, *Religious Lyrics of the XVth Century* (Oxford, 1939), pp. 102–3.

[120] Harley 5398, f. 20v; *Supplement*, No. 995.3; previously unpublished.

> Goddys chosyn who so wil be,
> And euer wony on his blis,
> Of viij rosis then most he
> A glorious garland make y-wis.
> Thynk al thi gilte, ofte hit wepe,
> Wil do no more thyn enemy þou loue,
> Thynk on þe deth, drede paynes depe,
> Aske mercy, haue blis a-boue.

In grammatical collections the manuscript researcher may light on an unpublished text of the *Parce michi Domine* lyric, the Bird with the Four Feathers, in a Latin *verbale*.[121] Or he may find the message of the song of the nightingale, delightful even if an exercise in translation:[122]

> þe ny3tyngale synges
> þat all þe wod rynges;
> Scho singyth in here song
> þat þe ny3t is to long.

Or in a composite collection of school texts on grammar, an added exercise, followed by the Latin translation:[123]

> When the clot klyngueth,
> and þe cucko synguth,
> and þe brome sprynguth,
> then his tyme a 3ongeling
> forto go a-wowyng.

In prognostics the manuscript researcher may find a complaint, 'Alas, howe schale my hert be lyght, / Wyth dart of loue when hyt ys slayn', in the midst of a collection of prophecies and astrology in Latin, English, and Welsh.[124]

[121] Bodl. Lat. Misc. E. 85, ff. 79r–81r (9 st.); *Supplement*, No. 561; unpublished.

[122] NLW Peniarth 356, p. 196; *Supplement*, No. 3439.5; pr. Robbins, *Anglia*, LXXXIII. 46.

[123] Harley 1002, f. 102v; *Supplement*, No. 4028.6; pr. C. E. Wright, 'Late ME Parerga in a School Collection', *RES*, n.s. II (1951), 119.

[124] NLW Peniarth 26, p. 108; *Index*, No. 152; pr. Robbins, *Secular Lyrics of the XIVth and XVth Centuries*, rev. ed. (Oxford, 1955), pp. 152–3.

In medical manuscripts the manuscript researcher may run
across an ale wives' poem which tells of real women, who can be
identified from financial records in other parts of the manuscript.
They are described sitting in the local, christening their new loving
cup:[125]

> pes, mersy, and scharyte—
> þis be þe potes name al iij.
> When pes Is In bed I-brought,
> And mersy is after sought,
> Scharyte most com behend
> And ellys wyll nought be þi frend.

He may look at Henry Daniel's treatise on urines, and be surprised
to find stanzas on the Three Worthies, Caesar, Alexander, and
Hector, perhaps intended as tapestry verses:[126]

> I Iulius cesare, ȝour hegh emperour,
> In fryth and in feld full faire was my fame;
> Of Rome and romans I bare ay þe floure,
> and þus capud mundi was I called be name.

In commonplace books the manuscript researcher may turn up
poems of unexpected beauty. In a largely astrological collection
(about 1425–50) occurs an alliterative poem in a curious nine-line
stanza form, 'Stirps beate Anne'.[127] In a commonplace book of
heraldic materials is a hitherto unknown text of Skelton's poem on
Time.[128]

It amounts to this: a scholar never knows what assignation

---

[125] Harley 1735, f. 48r; *Supplement*, No. 870.8; edition pending.

[126] Wellcome Hist. Med. Mus. 225, f. 2v; *Supplement*, No. 1322.5; unpub-
lished. These three stanzas are apparently an earlier version of the poem on the
Nine Worthies, *Supplement*, No. 1270.1, added to a 1488 printed book in
Corpus Christi Coll. Oxf., and pr. Milne and Sweeting, *MLR*, XL (1945), 87–9.

[127] Aberdeen Univ. 123, f. 131v; *Supplement*, No 2153.5; unpublished. I am
currently preparing editions of most of the unpublished shorter poems noted in
this essay.

[128] Trinity Coll. Dublin 661, pp. 3–5 (st. 7, 9, 10, 11 only); *Supplement*, No.
2451.5; unpublished.

c

awaits him between the sheets; he may have one lean day, but he will be compensated later. Even looking through a technical prose treatise, like a *Maister of the Game*, he will turn the page and without warning read a charming informal lyric to 'myne nown good mastres', printed quite a number of years ago. Here is the first of its five stanzas:[129]

> My loue so swyte
> Iesu kype
> > Where soo euer that yow be;
> all for yowere sake
> my harte dothe schake,
> > and sore hyt gryvys me.

Such is the interplay between pure and practical literature in ME manuscripts. Both give mirth. In fact, the fun of research is more fun than fun.

[129] Sloane 3501, f. 52v; *Supplement*, No. 2261.6; pr. Bernhard Fehr, 'Weitere Beiträge zur englischen Lyrik', *Archiv*, CVII (1901), 52–3.

II

Caxton and Courtly Style

N. F. BLAKE

IN this paper I should like to consider how Caxton reacted to contemporary trends in literary English and what information this
yields us about the development of fifteenth-century English
prose. Those who have commented on Caxton's attitude to the
literary language have usually been content to review the opinions
found in his prologue to *Eneydos*. But *Eneydos* was one of the last
books he printed, and the prologue represents the culmination of
his views about English which had been developing over the
previous twenty years. Consequently a juster appreciation of
Caxton's attitude towards English may be obtained by examining
his prologues and epilogues in the order in which they were
written, for not only are his final views of interest, but also the
influences which caused his opinions to change in the way they did
are important for an understanding of the fifteenth century. So I
shall commence by tracing briefly the development of his opinions.

We must naturally start with the *History of Troy*, the first
English book to be printed. In his various prologues to this work,
Caxton claimed that he took pleasure in the 'fayr langage of
Frenshe' (4),[1] for the original was written 'in prose so well and
compendiously sette and wreton, whiche me thought I vnderstood
the sentence and substance of euery mater' (4). When he had
completed some of his translation he showed it to Margaret of
Burgundy who found fault with his English. What criticism she
made is not revealed, though it is more than likely she thought
the style not sufficiently ornate. As it was, Caxton claimed that he
followed the original as closely as he could, but nevertheless the

---

[1] The references in brackets after Caxtonian quotations are to pages in
W. J. B. Crotch, *The Prologues and Epilogues of William Caxton*, EETS o.s. 176
(London, 1928). I have, however, modernized the punctuation.

result was a 'rude werk' (5) containing 'rude Englissh' (6). The impression one gets is that Caxton followed the French closely in order to share the merits of its style which was so 'compendious' and intelligible, but that unfortunately something was lost in the process of translation. No doubt some of this attitude is conventional for it was traditional to decry one's own merits by employing the humility formula. But both the praise of French style and the words used to express that praise are important. Caxton praises French prose, but mentions no English prose as being comparable. Yet the word 'compendious', which he uses to describe French prose style, was a favourite one with Lydgate, as a few examples will show:

Undir a stile breeff & compendious (*Fall of Princes* I. 90)
Compendiously this mateer for to declare (ibid. VIII. 2647)
Withoute frute he was compendious (*Troy-Book* Prol. 351)
Now must I ful besy ben a whyle . . .
Myn auctor folwe & be compendious (ibid. V. 2315-19).

Conciseness was not in fact a virtue of the French original or Caxton's translation, or even indeed of Lydgate. But it was evidently considered a necessary virtue of style. The term was used by Lydgate to describe his own poetic style. It was adapted by Caxton to the French prose style of his original in order to show that it had the same stylistic features as English poetry. It was these features which he wished to give to his own prose by close translation. The quotations from Lydgate's *Troy-Book* are important for Caxton knew this work, to which he refers in his prologue. But he refers to it in tones of the greatest respect. His own translation, he writes, cannot in any way be compared with Lydgate's poem though it covers much of the same ground. Caxton completed his translation only because his own was in prose.

After his return to England Caxton printed the *Dicts of Philosophers* translated by Earl Rivers and his own translation of *Jason*. While the latter repeats that Caxton's translations have little in the way of elegant prose, in the prologue to the former Caxton wanted to pay Rivers a compliment on his translation. To us today there seems little difference stylistically between the two, though Caxton speaks of them in quite different ways. The one has no 'beaute or good endyting of our Englissh tonge' (34), the other is 'right wel & connyngly made & translated into right good and fayr Englissh' (20). The important thing to notice is the paucity of Caxton's critical vocabulary. He has neglected to use 'compendious' and there is no reference to rhetoric. He has not yet learned how to praise a work. This he was to do by printing Chaucer's *Boethius*, for through this work he became aware of the critical opinions about Chaucer common in the fifteenth century. There is a significant enlargement of Caxton's critical vocabulary in the prologue to this book. Chaucer was the 'first translatour of this sayde boke into Englissh & enbelissher in making the sayd langage ornate & fayr' (37). The 'langage' appears to mean English in general rather than the prose of the translation, for Chaucer is also called 'the worshipful fader & first foundeur & enbelissher of ornate eloquence in our Englissh' (37). It has been shown that Caxton took these phrases from other works about Chaucer which were known to him.[1] Caxton is absorbing the fashion current at the time, in which the two words 'ornate' and 'embellisher' appear constantly.[2] Nevertheless we should not forget that Chaucer is also praised for following the Latin 'as neygh as is possible to be vnderstande' (37). The same point is made in *Of Old Age*. The Latin text, in which matters are 'specyfyced compendiously' (42), is difficult, but 'this book, reduced in Englyssh tongue, is more ample expowned and more swetter to the reder, kepyng the iuste sentence of the Latyn' (42).

Trevisa's translation of Higden's *Polychronicon* was treated differently. Although made within ten years of Chaucer's *Boethius*, this translation was considered by Caxton to be outdated, though good. Consequently he has 'chaunged the rude and old Englyssh, that is to wete certayn wordes which in these dayes be neither vsyd ne vnderstanden' (68). Trevisa evidently did not have

[1] N. F. Blake, 'Caxton and Chaucer', *Leeds Studies in English*, i (1967), 19-36.
[2] C. F. E. Spurgeon, *Five Hundred Years of Chaucer Criticism and Allusion*, I. 1357-1800 (London, 1914).

quite the same stylistic reputation as Chaucer and therefore his
language wanted modernization. As a close translation of Higden
it was estimable, but it wanted some embellishment.

With his second edition of *Canterbury Tales* Caxton repeats
many of the critical comments he had made about Chaucer in his
prologue to *Boethius*. Chaucer embellished English and made it
ornate. But Caxton now also mentions what had been characteristic of English prior to Chaucer. Then the English language
was 'rude' and 'incongrue, as yet it appiereth by olde bookes' (90).
Whether these old books were in poetry or prose is not revealed.
But there is a clear indication that Chaucer polished English by
making it rhetorical and ornate as one can see by comparing his
writings with older books. Caxton goes on to praise Chaucer for
his conciseness and his 'sugred eloquence' (90), the sentiments and
the words being alike borrowed from Lydgate.[1] Caxton has
become more deeply involved in the current critical fashions
about Chaucer and court poetry.

At this stage his involvement begins to affect his descriptions of
his own prose. He has become aware of what is expected in a good
style. In *Charles the Great* he uses the critical vocabulary of
rhetoric to comment on his own translation for the first time. He
is still, as usual, apologetic for his style which he calls 'rude &
symple reducyng' (96). But he goes a step further by commenting
on the lack of rhetoric: 'though so be there be no gaye termes ne
subtyl ne newe eloquence, yet I hope that it shal be vnderstonden'
(96). His association with the court and his knowledge of Chaucerian criticism must have made him conscious of what was
fashionable. Yet he still attaches importance to comprehension as
well as to decoration, a point to which he returns: 'And yf in al
thys book I haue mesprysed or spoken otherwyse than good
langage substancyally ful of good vnderstondyng to al makers and
clerkes, I demaunde correxyon and amendement' (98). It seems as
though a good style and comprehensibility go hand in hand. From
now on an apology for the absence of the gay terms of rhetoric 'as
now be sayd in these dayes and vsed' (105) is a constant feature of
his prologues. It is found particularly in *Feats of Arms* and

[1] Blake, op. cit.

Blanchardyn and Eglantine. Quotation from these hardly seems necessary. Yet he still goes on insisting that he has followed his French source closely and uttering the hope that his works are comprehensible.

The discussion of rhetoric in the prologue to *Eneydos* is the natural culmination of the other prologues. In some ways Caxton has not changed. He still translates because of the style of his French original: 'in whiche booke I had grete playsyr by cause of the fayr and honest termes & wordes in Frenshe, whyche I neuer sawe to fore lyke ne none so playsaunt ne so wel ordred' (107). The difference is now that he has a greater stock of words with which to express his pleasure. He admits, however, that there are some gentlemen who have taken objection to his translations because he used 'ouer curyous termes whiche coude not be vnderstande of comyn people' and they wanted him to use 'olde and homely termes' (108). This fact is interesting in showing that Caxton's opinions were influenced by the fashion of the court and also that there was an anti-rhetorical faction at court. Caxton goes on to say that he read an old book which he found difficult to understand because of its 'rude and brood' English. Similarly at the request of the Abbot of Westminster he looked at some old documents whose language was more like 'Dutch' (i.e. Low German) than English so that he was unable to understand it. This leads Caxton on to the everchanging nature of the English language, an opinion which he may well have picked up from the poets of the courtly tradition.[1] The implication of his argument is that those who wish for the old and homely terms are foolish, for English has progressed beyond that state whether they like it or not. He prefers modern terminology since his books are designed for a cultivated and educated audience. However, he will try to maintain a middle position between the extremes of old and homely terms and over-refinement. But significantly he refers those who fail to understand his language to Virgil and the *Epistles* of Ovid, from which one can assume that he was on the side of the educated, Latinate clientele and that he thought his rhetorical embellishments were based on Latin. Finally, Caxton

[1] Cf. *Confessio Amantis*, Prol. 142, *Troilus and Criseyde* II. 22–5.

praises the work of John Skelton extravagantly. Since Skelton was one of the most prominent aureate writers of the time, it confirms that Caxton was in favour of rhetoric and embellishment and it suggests that he wanted his own work to be judged by such standards.

Now that this survey of Caxton's views is complete, it is time to evaluate the points arising from it. The most important is the evidence that at the start of his publishing career he had little critical vocabulary, but that he enlarged this vocabulary over the years. The two major influences contributing to this increase were the critical opinions surrounding the works of Chaucer and the opinions of his fashionable clientele from the court. The greatest impetus within the former influence came undoubtedly from the works of Lydgate, since Lydgate followed what he thought was the Chaucerian poetic tradition and wrote many lines in his praise. Indeed there is much to suggest that Caxton looked at Chaucer through the works of Lydgate. But the Chaucerian criticism was directed more to the poetic language than to English in general. Caxton was forced to follow the poetic model even though he was writing in prose, because the new poetic style had such prestige and because there was no English prose in the courtly style which he could emulate. To some extent the absence of such a prose style was beginning to be rectified at the end of Caxton's life by the works of Skelton, and clearly a court which contained such an aureate writer as Skelton as tutor to the Prince of Wales could hardly avoid being concerned with rhetorical fashion. This in its turn would influence Caxton. But in general the absence of a native prose style was overcome by translating from Latin or French and by following the original style closely. This is why Caxton constantly refers us to the French and Latin originals. Their style has those features which English prose lacks, but which could be found in English poetry. At the same time there was in existence in English an older prose style, which was not considered a satisfactory model, just as there had been an older poetic style which had been outmoded by the Chaucerian revolution. That style could be seen in old books. Exactly what this style consisted of is not clear, since Caxton never discusses the matter in detail, though the general history of late medieval English literature leads me to accept that it was the alliterative style. For Caxton the disadvantages of this old style were its vocabulary and lack of rhetorical refinement. Old books used an obsolete vocabulary, they used words no longer fashionable. Presumably they were words of Anglo-Saxon or Norse origin instead of being modern words coined from French or Latin. Similarly the old books followed the native stylistic traditions instead of following the rhetoric found in French or Latin models.

So far I have been considering Caxton's developing attitude to style and rhetoric, and the influences which caused that attitude to change. Now it is necessary to consider to what extent Caxton's own style was influenced by the fashionable acceptance of rhetoric. Wendelstein,[1] for example, has pointed to some minor rhetorical flourishes in Caxton's *Charles the Great*. Thus he notes the repetition of the suffix *-ly* at the end of clauses: 'and dyd do paynte the hystoryes after somme poyntes of our crysten fayth moche ryche*ly* and repayred the places ryght delycyous*ly*. And on that other he dyd do ordeyne & founde chirches autentyk*ly*, & compose baptyzatoryes & frentes conuenab*ly*' (fol. a8ᵛ). He also singles out the pointing of clauses by the use of rhyming words: 'Whan thys was de*maunded*, it was com*maunded*' (fol. b6ᵛ). But Wendelstein omitted to mention that these rhetorical tricks are taken over directly from the French *Fierabras*, which Caxton was translating: (i) 'puys a paindre histoires selon aulcuns poins de nostre foy cristienne moult riche*ment* et les places reparer tres delicieuse*ment*, et d'aultre part il fist ordonner et fonder esglises auctentique*ment* et composer baptitoires conuenable*ment*' (fol. b1ʳ); (ii) 'Cecy estre de*mandé*, il fut com*mandé*' (fol. b8ʳ). Here we should recall that one of Caxton's major theses was that English prose style was at its best when it kept as close as possible to a French or Latin original. He insisted on this because it was intended that some of the fine French or Latin style would show through in the English translation. It should not, therefore, be a matter for surprise that this did in fact happen from time to time. It does not of course follow that Caxton was aware of all the places where this had

[1] L. Wendelstein, *Beitrag zur Vorgeschichte des Euphuismus* (Halle, 1902), p. 4.

taken place. And it is certainly true that his own original compositions cannot be shown to have been influenced by foreign models. No rhetorical flourishes have been pointed out in his own compositions, which are more notable for their clumsy style than for their balanced or rhythmical sentences.[1] His style becomes very loose when he has no guide. His appreciation of rhetoric is superficial: he was unable to practise what he preached. The one exception could be his use of doublets, which was a type of embellishment. This feature had been used by Chaucer, and is largely confined in Caxton to passages which demand a more elevated style. They allow Caxton to use French loanwords and thus to give his work a more fashionable appearance. The French content of Caxton's vocabulary depends likewise on whether the passage is translated or original. Original passages contain far fewer loanwords than translated ones, though they do not have words from the alliterative style. His own prose uses a limited vocabulary, though he does use words which were no doubt fashionable such as 'noble'.[2] Neither his style nor his vocabulary was particularly affected by French when he made an original composition. Furthermore we should realize that his policy of translating closely from Latin or French was one which he probably adopted because it was the fashion of the time to do so. He did it, he says, to transfer the elegances of French and Latin style to English. Yet he also translated closely when he translated from Flemish, as in *Reynard the Fox*, which meant he imported many Flemish loanwords. Yet since in his prologue to *Eneydos* he stated that the older English, which he was trying to avoid, and Low German had much in common, one might have supposed that he would have avoided imitating Flemish style and introducing Flemish loanwords. He did not; and once again we see that Caxton did not carry out in his own work what he claimed as desirable. This inability to carry out his own stated preferences is important in confirming that his opinions reflect contemporary ideas rather

[1] R. R. Aurner, 'Caxton and the English Sentence', *University of Wisconsin Studies in Language and Literature*, xviii (1923), 23–59.

[2] N. F. Blake, 'Caxton's Language', *Neuphilologische Mitteilungen,* lxvii (1966), 122–32.

than his own observations and practice. This is why his evidence is so valuable.

Even though Caxton may not have been able to provide much in the way of rhetorical embellishment in his individual compositions, one would expect contemporary prejudices to manifest themselves in his choice of texts for he would have to sell them to his fashionable clientele. Although my subject is prose rather than poetry, the evidence from the poetry is important and I shall deal briefly with that first. The major poets printed by Caxton are Chaucer, Gower and Lydgate, and these three represent the triumvirate of the courtly tradition. Their names were constantly linked by fifteenth-century and early sixteenth-century writers who commented on the new poetic fashion. All the other poetry printed by Caxton may be said to be part of this new tradition. Benedict Burgh was Lydgate's pupil and finished some of his work; the *Court of Sapience* was often attributed to Lydgate himself; and the poet of the *Book of Courtesy* looks back to Chaucer, Gower and Lydgate as the three great poets and thus reveals his allegiance. All the poems use stanza or couplet, a markedly French vocabulary and many rhetorical expedients. On the other hand, Caxton has often been blamed for not printing *Piers Plowman*. Since so many manuscripts of this poem circulated in the fifteenth century, and since some of them were connected with London, it seems likely that Caxton knew of its existence. We cannot be certain about this, but we can imagine that if he did know of the poem he would not have printed it, for it must have represented to him the older poetic tradition from which Chaucer had broken away. It uses the old alliterative metre with old words arranged in the traditional English manner. In terms of poetry Caxton must have meant the alliterative poems when he referred to 'old books'.

It would be natural to assume that Caxton and his contemporaries were affected by the current fashion towards poetry in their attitude to prose. As far as Caxton is concerned, this would mean that we would expect him to publish work in the courtly stylistic tradition and to avoid the alliterative or native prose. This assumption may be tested firstly by considering what type of prose work

Caxton chose to print and secondly by examining how he edited the books before printing them. The characteristic feature of the prose printed by Caxton is that it consists either of translation or of work based on foreign models. I must emphasize that I am not here concerned with Caxton's own translations, but only with those works which already existed in an English version before coming into Caxton's hands. Such works include Earl Rivers's two translations, *Dicts of Philosophers* and *Cordial*; Chaucer's translation of *Boethius*; Worcester's translations, *Declamation of Noblesse* and *Of Friendship*; the earlier English translation of *Of Old Age;* Trevisa's translation of Higden's *Polychronicon*, with which we may include the *Description of Britain*; and Malory's *Morte Darthur*. This book we today tend to think of as a re-creation rather than a translation, but to Caxton it was 'take oute of certayn bookes of Frensshe and reduced' (94) to English. The above list is in no way comprehensive, for it excludes many of the more specifically religious works, such as *Mirror of the Life of Christ* and *Pilgrimage of the Soul*. All these are translations as well, except for Mirk's *Festial* which is a re-telling of the *Legenda Aurea* rather than a straightforward translation. Of all the publications issuing from the press only one can properly be said not to be a translation, namely the *Chronicles of England*. And this work, which originated as a translation and for which there were foreign models, is closely associated with London and the court. It has no trace of the alliterative style. What is noticeable, therefore, about Caxton's choice of books is that he did not print anything by an Englishman written in what we may call the native tradition. Such authors as Rolle, Hilton and the author of the *Cloud of Unknowing* are completely passed over, even though their works were popular and many manuscripts survived. Though sometimes modelled on foreign sources, the works of these authors can hardly be thought of as translations. And more importantly they belong stylistically to the native prose tradition.[1] Furthermore,

[1] There has been some discussion as to whether there were several styles in Middle English prose, e.g. E. Zeeman, 'Continuity in Middle English Devotional Prose', *Journal of English and Germanic Philology*, lv (1956), 417–22. But as Caxton does not discriminate between varieties of the old style, I have regarded alliteration as the style he was referring to.

even such original English compositions as there were in the fifteenth century were not printed by Caxton. There can consequently be no doubt that Caxton favoured translated works and that this prejudice was shared by many members of the court. The most cultivated and respected men of the time, such as Rivers, Worcester, Skelton and later Berners—to name only a few— made translations rather than original compositions. It is significant that the only works by Skelton which Caxton referred to are all translations: 'For he hath late translated the Epystlys of Tulle, and the boke of Dyodorus Syculus, and diuerse other werkes oute of Latyn in to Englysshe' (109).

It is not difficult to understand how this prejudice came about. In the fifteenth century the distinction between poetry and prose was not so great as it is now. It was accepted that poetry had broken out of the old mould by using foreign models. Chaucer had modelled his poems on French or Italian ones, and Gower had made good use of Ovid. Lydgate had made many poetic 'translations', of which his *Troy-Book* is perhaps the outstanding example. Though we today tend to highlight Lydgate's statements that he was writing in the Chaucerian tradition, we should not forget that he also in the *Troy-Book* pays many fulsome tributes to Guido's style. It was natural that prose should follow the lead set by poetry; that it should emancipate itself from the native tradition by following foreign models. But there was one important difference. In poetry there had been Chaucer; in prose there was no English model of comparable stature. Therefore while Lydgate and other fifteenth-century poets could claim to be writing in the Chaucerian manner, although more often than not they were imitating foreign models, the prose writers could not claim to be following any English model. Hence they were thrown back on their sources which they tended to follow slavishly. It is of course easier to be more literal in prose, and we may notice that even poets such as Chaucer and Skelton made literal prose translations. But it is the great misfortune of late medieval English prose that neither Skelton nor Chaucer established himself as a model. This meant that there was no English model which could curb the worst excesses of translation and make the translator lift his eyes from his source.

We must now consider the other aspect of Caxton's publishing activity, namely to what extent he altered the texts he had decided to print. In many cases it is not possible to come to any decision since his version is the only one that survives. But from what he wrote in his prologues it would seem unlikely that he altered the translations by, say, Rivers or Worcester. Similarly he did not materially change Chaucer's *Boethius*. These translations were not touched because Caxton had too much respect for the translators. There are, however, two works which Caxton did alter considerably, Malory's *Morte Darthur* and Trevisa's translation of Higden. The reasons which led Caxton to adapt these works differ; but it is better first to discuss what the changes were before considering what caused them.

From even a glance at Vinaver's edition of Malory,[1] it is evident that Caxton altered Book Five most. This is the book which is based upon the English alliterative poem, *Le Morte Arthure*, and Malory took over much of the vocabulary and alliteration. Let us consider a short passage from this book together with Caxton's adaptation:

> *Malory:* Than the kynge yode up to the creste of the cragge, and than he comforted hymself with the colde wynde; and than he yode forth by two welle-stremys, and there he fyndys two fyres flamand full hygh. And at that one fyre he founde a carefull wydow wryngande hir handys syttande on a grave that was new marked. Than Arthur salued hir and she hym agayne, and asked hir why she sate sorowyng. 'Alas,' she seyde, 'carefull knyght. Thou carpys over lowde! Yon is a werlow woll destroy us bothe.'
>
> *Caxton:* And soo he ascended up in to that hylle tyl he came to a grete fyre, and there he fonde a careful wydowe wryngynge

---

[1] E. Vinaver, *The Works of Sir Thomas Malory* (Oxford, 1947). Both passages quoted below are from this edition, p. 200. For a discussion of Malory's language and Caxton's handling of it see Sally Shaw, 'Caxton and Malory' in *Essays on Malory*, edited by J. A. W. Bennett (Oxford, 1963), pp. 114–45; and W. Matthews, *The Ill-Framed Knight* (Berkeley and Los Angeles, 1966).

her handes and makyng grete sorowe, syttynge by a grave new made. And thenne kynge Arthur salewed her and demaunded of her wherefore she made such lamentacion. To whom she ansuerd and sayd: 'Syre knyghte, speke softe for yonder is a devyll; yf he here the speke, he wyll come and destroye the.'

In the Caxton passage we may note the avoidance of alliterative groups: *creste of the cragge, comforted . . . colde, fyres flamand, sate sorowyng, carefull knyght*. Some of the alliteration may have been eliminated incidentally through the attempt to modernize the vocabulary. It is interesting to see how often this modernization takes the form of introducing French words: *ascended* (*yode up*), *demaunded* (*asked*), *lamentacion* (*sorowyng*); though in other cases it merely involves using a less specific word for the forceful older word: *devyll* (*werlow*), *speke* (*carpys*). Caxton also uses vague adjectives such as 'great' as in '*grete* fyre' and '*grete* sorowe'. The tone of the conversations has become more elevated in Caxton, for not only does the lady address Arthur as 'Syre knyghte', but her speech is also more subdued from the brusque tone it has in Malory. In general Caxton's version is more courtly and less specific. Finally we may note the use of repetition in 'wryngynge her handes and makyng grete sorowe', in which the latter phrase has been added by Caxton. The use of the doublet may have been an attempt by Caxton to heighten the pathos by using a rhetorical figure. The changes I have pointed to show how Caxton adapted the text. It is significant that the passage should be from the fifth book. The remaining books, which are for the most part based on French sources, are generally only modified rather than rewritten.

Trevisa's translation was different from Malory's. It was an older English translation of a standard Latin work by a man who had achieved some eminence as a translator. Caxton, for example, also mentions his translations of the Bible and *De Proprietatibus Rerum*. Nevertheless, Caxton felt that Trevisa's language should be modernized. As with Malory, these changes often involved the introduction of French words: *embelysshers* (*hiȝteres*), *encrece* (*eche*), *doctryne* (*lore*), *obedient* (*buxom*), *disposed* (*icast*), though in many cases we find the replacement of one Germanic word by another: *calleth* (*clepeth*), *after* (*efte*), *dyches* (*meres*), *right* (*swipe*).[1] Yet there is a difference in Caxton's attitude towards these two authors. Trevisa made use of alliteration in his translation, but more often than not the alliteration is confined within a doublet. Caxton has not altered these doublets as a general rule so that such expressions as *halkes and huyrenes* and *wayes and wrynclis* remain. The reason for this is twofold. Trevisa's alliteration is a stylistic ornament superimposed upon the basic sentence pattern, which is solidly based on Higden's Latin. In Malory's Book Five, on the other hand, the alliteration is an integral part of the sentence structure and any recasting of the sentence results in destroying the alliteration. But in Trevisa the alliteration, being decorative, occurs in doublets and the revision of any sentence would not necessarily lead to its elimination. And Caxton, as we have seen, was partial to doublets. Indeed one of the notable features of his adaptation of Trevisa is the increase in their number.[2] Furthermore, doublets had been used by Chaucer and other courtly writers, so that in Chaucer's *Boethius* we find such pairs as *commoevynge and chasynge, duskid and dirked, felonyes and fraudes*. Thus Trevisa must have had many stylistic virtues in Caxton's eyes, even though his vocabulary was not sufficiently modern. It would seem as though Caxton thought Trevisa, though an older writer, less old-fashioned than Malory.[3]

Certainly Caxton would also have considered Malory more old-fashioned than Chaucer. But how would he have regarded Trevisa in relation to Chaucer? Both men were translating at approximately the same time. Yet Caxton claimed that Trevisa's language was no longer up to date, whereas he has nothing but praise for Chaucer's. In so far as the matter has been studied, it would seem that Caxton made few alterations to Chaucer's

[1] Not much work on Caxton's treatment of Trevisa's language has been done, but see C. Babington, *Polychronicon Ranulphi Higden Monachi Cestrensis*, vol. I (London, 1865), pp. lxiii–lxviii, and B. L. Kinkade, *The English Translations of Higden's Polychronicon* (Urbana, 1932).

[2] Kinkade, op. cit., p. 20.

[3] We should not forget that Caxton thought so highly of Trevisa that he kept his own continuation apart from Trevisa's work; see Crotch, p. 68.

prose.[1] Caxton allows such words as *yclepid* and *apayed*, which he frequently altered for his printing of Trevisa, to remain in Chaucer's text. There are not, however, many such words in Chaucer, for his language is definitely more Latinate and his style more ornate than Trevisa's. This difference is attributable to the different areas in which they lived and possibly the tastes of their patrons. Chaucer's association with the court and London no doubt influenced his style. Trevisa wrote his work in the West Country which was less affected by courtly fashions. It would seem as though Caxton viewed Chaucer, Trevisa and Malory in that descending order of stylistic excellence. This order also represents the extent to which he modified their translations. Furthermore, he did recognize the differences between various styles, and he considered style sufficiently important to justify his rectifying what was not fashionable.

The preceding survey has necessarily been brief, but it has shown that Caxton attempted to print works written in what he considered to be the courtly style and that when a book was not written in that style, he altered it to make it conform. There can also be little doubt that he acted in this way because he was attempting to follow the fashion of the court. This conclusion leads to some further observations. Today we tend to think that modern prose style originated with Malory. To Caxton and the fifteenth century it must have seemed as though Malory was the culmination of the old, alliterative style: he represented the end of one style rather than the beginning of another. It is time now that we reconsidered the position of the fifteenth century in the history of English prose, for we have hitherto failed to recognize that the authors of the time were trying to break new ground. Consequently their achievement has been undervalued. They could see that poetry had made a new start and they wished to do the same for prose. But since they had no English model and were forced to rely on foreign ones, it is only to be expected that their attempts to fashion a new style should seem naïve to us. But this does not mean that the fifteenth-century translator 'had seldom any

---

[1] A start was made by L. Kellner, 'Zur Textkritik von Chaucer's Boethius', *Englische Studien*, xiv (1890), 1–52.

D

interest in English style'.[1] On the contrary, he was intensely conscious of it and tried to improve it. Naturally the first steps were uncertain, but the fifteenth-century translators paved the way for the achievements of the sixteenth century. And if Berners is the first to write modern English prose, it was only because many before him had shown him the way. But this does not mean that there was such a straight line of descent from early medieval English prose to Renaissance prose, as some writers on Middle English prose have suggested.[2] Of course, the translators were influenced by the alliterative tradition which they were trying to supersede. And we have seen that some alliteration was acceptable. But the fifteenth century was trying to make a definite break with the prose of the past, and they were to a large extent successful. Modern scholars have tended to minimize this break because insufficient attention has been paid to the works and aims of fifteenth-century translators.

Finally, I should like to consider whether the attitudes to prose I have traced in the fifteenth century might have any bearing upon our views of the Alliterative Revival, though here I can do no more than make one or two general suggestions. There is a tendency to link the revival with the north and west of the country, and even to suggest that it might have been fostered by baronial opposition to the central monarchy.[3] For Caxton and the fifteenth century the alliterative style in both prose and poetry represented the old English style for the whole country. Chaucer had broken away from it in poetry and many fifteenth-century disciples had followed in his footsteps. Similarly prose writers had tried to adapt his stylistic revolution to prose by basing their work on foreign models. The new style was associated with London and the court. Yet even there in the fifteenth century there were

---

[1] I. A. Gordon, *The Movement of English Prose* (London, 1966), p. 64.

[2] See, for example, R. W. Chambers, *On the Continuity of English Prose* (London, 1957) and M. W. Croll, 'The Sources of the Euphuistic Rhetoric', reprinted in *Style, Rhetoric, and Rhythm*, ed. by J. M. Patrick and R. O. Evans (Princeton, 1966), 241–95.

[3] J. R. Hulbert, 'A Hypothesis concerning the Alliterative Revival', *Modern Philology*, xxviii (1931), 405–22. But see more recently E. Salter, 'The Alliterative Revival', *Modern Philology*, lxiv (1966–7), 146–50; 233–7.

still people who favoured the old alliterative tradition and who wanted Caxton to follow that style. Wynkyn de Worde did in fact revert to the older style by publishing the works of such authors as Rolle. These two facts show that the old style was still popular in London and elsewhere, and that it was the Chaucerian style which was new and trying to break away. For many in London the alliterative style must still have been the accepted one. Chaucer and his followers were the innovators, not the alliterative writers. This, I suggest, is how the fifteenth century saw the relationship of the two styles. And if they saw it in this way, it could well be that this was what in fact had happened. Certainly it seems unlikely that, if the alliterative style was characteristic only of the North and West, there would have been sufficient adherents of the style in London to make Caxton give it serious attention.

I hope I have shown that Caxton can tell us a great deal about contemporary literary fashion. Caxton is important because he is one of the few people who discuss what they are trying to do. Too many other fifteenth-century authors have merely left translations without giving us any insight into their method of working. Caxton tells us why he produced certain works and at the same time, as he is not himself a literary innovator, he reveals what others were thinking as well. This evidence has been overlooked in the past, but I would venture to suggest that it is of crucial importance for an understanding of the development of fifteenth-century English prose.

III

The Measure of 'Comus'

PHILIP BROCKBANK

A Mask Presented at Ludlow Castle (to recall Milton's own title) has endured a great weight of commentary in recent years, and there is some excuse for fearing that another butterfly is being broken on a wheel. But the case is therefore the fitter for discussion. *Comus* still casts its instant spell upon the attentive (however uninitiated) spectator and reader; it is still one of the more available minor masterpieces of the past, whatever it may offer to esoteric exegesis. Taking advantage of a survey recently offered by Marjorie Hope Nicolson in *A Reader's Guide to John Milton* (1964), we may notice that the most significant divergence of views on *Comus* is between those who, following A. S. P. Woodhouse,[1] see it as a vehicle for mystic and theological truths about the state of nature and the state of grace, and those who (like Miss Nicolson herself) are satisfied with an entertainment in which, by convention, Virtue triumphs over Vice. Commentary continues to range from the gay acerbities of R. M. Adams[2] to the highly refined neo-platonic insights of Rosemond Tuve.[3] The need, as I see it, is to relate the apparently easy and familiar response to the apparently over-sophisticated or over-cultivated one. I wish to claim that the masque will only compose itself into a sustained and self-consistent whole, satisfying to the ethical imagination, when we have tuned our ears to certain effects ('List mortals if your ears be

---

[1] 'The Argument of Milton's *Comus*' and '*Comus* Once More', *University of Toronto Quarterly*, XI (1941), and XIX (1950).

[2] *Ikon: John Milton and the Modern Critics* (1955). Adams hopes that 'when the critics have learned a little temperance in the application of their Byzantine ingenuities, we shall be able to enjoy without apology the simple beauties of obvious commonplaces set in musical language'.

[3] *Images and Themes in Five Poems by Milton* (1957). Miss Tuve remarks that R. M. Adams leaves us 'with a fairly thoughtless work for tired practical minds'.

true') and when we have accustomed our eyes to certain perspectives.

I would begin by speculating about a first, untutored, response to a reading of *Comus*. Unlike Rosemond Tuve, I would put a high value upon what she calls 'a reader's impressionistic report of his reactions'.[1] For without impressions there is no poetry, and without precision and fidelity of report there can be no criticism; historical evidence may qualify or even transform impressions, it may enrich and complicate them, or confound and confuse them, but it cannot be substituted for them. A first experience of Comus once belonged to the ballroom, now it belongs to the classroom or to the library, under pedagogic direction, and this circumstance alone does much to determine the nature of the impression. Even under such conditions we may, however, be fairly promptly struck by the feeling that we *ought* to admire it, and will read with muted factitious respect, with interludes of active boredom or hostility, and with periods of exhilaration and delight. If we read aloud and with a quick eye for imagined spectacle, the pleasure will be more positive—even, perhaps, where the sentiments are least congenial. But the probability is that we do not first read for pleasure but for an austerer purpose, and systematic study requires that we come to terms with the introductions and the commentaries. Asked to remember that Sabrina was a *numen fluminis*, that Alice Egerton played the lady, that Milton at Cambridge was skilled in prolusion, and that in this mode of thought *castitas* and *agape caritas* are related, we may well feel that to consult our own personal impressions of moral babble, sensual sties, chastity and grace would be premature and impertinent. But it is not our callow, ill-informed, and perhaps idiosyncratic or commonplace opinions that need to be reported, but rather the participation of the poem in the rhythms and metaphors of our living thought.

For thought does live by rhythm and metaphor, and if at first reading we catch some exhilaration and delight, it is with these captives that reflection and discussion begin:[2]

[1] In *Milton Studies in Honor of Harris Francis Fletcher* (1961), p. 212.
[2] Quotations from Milton are from the text edited by B. A. Wright for *Everyman's Library* (revised 1962).

> *Bacchus* that first from out the purple Grape
> Crushd the sweet poison of mis-used Wine,
> After the *Tuscan* Mariners transformed
> Coasting the *Tyrrhene* shore, as the winds listed,
> On *Circes* Iland fell (who knows not *Circe*
> The daughter of the Sun? whose charmed Cup
> Whoever tasted, lost his upright shape,
> And downward fell into a groveling Swine) (46–53)

The opportunities for comment here are formidable and fascinating: Milton invented the encounter between Bacchus and Circe; 'transformed' is a Latin use of the passive participle; Tyrrhenia in central Italy was named Etruria or Tuscia by the Romans; Circe was the daughter of Helios and Perse, and her island was called Aeaea.[1] The glosses, whatever their ultimate relevance, are initially intrusive and distracting. What Milton made hauntingly remote, the notes struggle to make familiar. But it is the remoteness that matters still; the spaciousness and mystery of the distance in Milton's lines between the words 'Bacchus' and 'fell'. Where are the mariners, and what are they doing? They are in that visionary Mediterranean that Marlowe and Milton created in English between them; and they are suspended in a state between heroic voyaging and free drifting:

> Coasting the Tyrrhene shore, as the winds listed.

Is it an ordeal or a privilege? It is a state of enchantment. When we first reach the word 'fell', it is innocently used to mean 'lighted upon', and it comes as a satisfying consummation of the sentence, a point of arrival. Milton is re-enacting the spell that transformed the Tuscan mariners; but he releases us from that exquisite marine trance with a parenthesis, disarmingly introduced with a Spenserian phrase, that restores the moral perspectives and gives a much less auspicious meaning to the word 'fell':

> And downward fell into a groveling Swine.

We are moved at once by a spell-binding, entrancing use of words,

---

[1] Glosses sampled from *Comus and other Poems* edited by W. Ball (1890), and from Henry J. Todd's edition of 1809.

and by a morally aware, critical use of them. The fall is both ex-
hilarating and catastrophic—it will be so again when Mulciber
falls in Book I of *Paradise Lost*:

> From Morn
> To Noon he fell, from Noon to dewy Eve,
> A Summers day. . . .

Some thirty lines on in the Attendant Spirit's prologue the verse
asks a different response and occasions a different kind of gloss:

> But first I must put off
> These my skie robes spun out of *Iris* Wooff,
> And take the Weeds and likeness of a Swain,
> That to the service of this house belongs,
> Who with his soft Pipe and smooth-dittied Song
> Well knows to still the wilde winds when they roar
> And hush the waving Woods. (82–8)

This might invite comment on the conventions of masquerade and
the commonplaces of allegory—telling why the spirit comes from
the sky, and why he assumes the disguise of a shepherd piper; why
the Bridgewater household employed a tutor skilled in music, and
why Milton thought of musicians and poets alike as shepherds, and
as instruments of spiritual and moral harmony. It is a good passage
too to remind us of the buoyant and familiar, but assured and dignified, tone of the masque as a domestic entertainment. But the
point of continuity with the earlier lines is in the enchantment, the
casting of spells in the last three lines. This is Orphic song (it is apt
to recall Shakespeare's 'Orpheus with his lute') resolving tensions,
composed and tranquil. The Attendant Spirit and Comus (son of
Circe) are in some sense rival enchanters; the one descended from
the sky, to take up the Shepherd's pipe; the other a fallen sub-deity
in the forest, heir to the charmed cup.

Now it is not usual to look at *Comus* as if it were about a choice
of enchanted states. It is more common to begin with the con-
frontation of Comus with the Lady, or more generally with the
rival claims of indulgence and abstinence, sensuality and rigour.

It is common to begin with the *argument*, in the most restricted sense—with the formalities of debate that Johnson indicted for lack of sprightliness. From this beginning it would be easy to recognize Milton the poet at odds with Milton the moralist; Marlowe, as it were, having it out with Bunyan. It is a short step to say that the devil has all the best tunes, and that Milton 'was a true Poet and of the Devil's party without knowing it'. Blake's infernal insights, indeed ('The lust of the goat is the bounty of God'; 'Damn braces. Bless relaxes'; 'Exuberance is Beauty'), may be seen to mediate between Comus's vision and the modern consciousness, in so far as this is hostile to a systematic morality of constraints.[1]

The choice of enchanted states owes its significance, however, to the larger fable, to the device of the masque, and its machinery. The performance opens with a sentence that encompasses both 'Regions milde of calm and serene Air' and men on earth who:

> Confin'd and pesterd in this pin-fold here
> Strive to keep up a frail and Feaverish being (7–8)

It may be poignantly true that few can altogether disown the aptness of that phrase 'frail and Feaverish being' or fail to recognize its fitness in a piece so largely about the intoxication of the senses by wine, fecundity and a virgin's vulnerability. But it is also true that the sentiment may accord well with the temper of the occasion—since for the duration of the entertainment we are heirs both to the wild wood and to Jove's court; we share with the Spirit the illusion of Olympian privilege.

The essential feat, accomplished by Milton and to be repeated by those who read him, is to hold this insight into our frail and feverish being in perspective. It is most obvious that Comus's victims lose all sense of proportion and see awry:

[1] In the Boston Museum of Fine Arts there is a set of Blake's water-colour illustrations to the masque in which the energies of the Brothers and the Attendant Spirit subdue Comus quite unequivocally; but Blake makes much of the passage (290–303) where the Shepherd-Comus tells of seeing the 'more than human' brothers 'plucking ripe clusters' from the vine; he can therefore allow the brothers a full measure of 'exuberance'.

And they, so perfet is their misery,
Not once perceive their foul disfigurement,
But boast themselves more comely than before
And all their friends and native home forget
To roul with pleasure in a sensual stie. (73–7)

But, encompassed by the wood, neither the lady nor her brothers can enjoy the comprehensive vision which is a prerogative of the Attendant Spirit and the audience.

The promptest and simplest question that we might ask about the large design of the masque is, what, if anything, does the wood signify?

> but their way
Lies through the perplext paths of this drear Wood ... (36–7)
> where else
Shall I inform my unacquainted feet
In the blind mazes of this tangl'd Wood? (178–80)
> such cooling fruit
As the kind hospitable Woods provide. (185–6)

The wood is actual enough as well as metaphoric; the story tells us that the Earl's children are on their way to the castle to see their father assume his 'new-intrusted sceptre'; and the rumour early got about that they were in fact once lost in the woods outside Ludlow. But what does the choice of a wood seem to suggest about the hazards of human life? It needs no knowledge of Dante to respond to the question: the darkness, the loss of direction, the unknown threats, the vulnerability of the innocent, together with the wood's consolations: the fruit, the coolness, and the glimpses of light. A little reflection, however, shows that within the masque the wood seems sometimes to signify the whole span of human life—the mortal state—and sometimes only a precarious phase of it. To be struck by the first possibility we need to recall what the Attendant Spirit says about 'mortal change', the 'Palace of Eternity' and 'the broad fields of the sky'; the wood in comparison is like the confining pinfold and the 'sin-worn mould' of the flesh; it is the condition of human life as a Platonizing Christian might see it. The other possibility—that it is a precarious phase of life—is the more conspicuous whenever the youth of the travellers is touched upon; as at the beginning:

> And here their tender age might suffer peril (40)

and at the end:

> *Heav'n hath timely tri'd their youth,*
> *Their faith, their patience, and their truth,*
> *And sent them here through hard assays*
> *With a crown of deathless Praise.* (969–72)

The masque, or entertainment, carries its moral burden lightly, and Milton makes it the prerogative of the form to hover daintily between possibilities of meaning. Nevertheless, it is crucial to recognize that the wood is an ordeal that the travellers triumphantly survive:

> *To triumph in victorious dance*
> *Ore sensual Folly and Intemperance.* (973–4)

We are free still to wonder whether this joyous state is terrestrial or extra-terrestrial, with a consummation in maturity or in death. The masque, playfully, has it both ways. And so it should. Music, dance, song and poetry together are best fitted both to preface a ball in a great seventeenth-century country house, and to offer intimations of a world rarer and finer than the one most familiar to our quotidian senses.

In so far as it is a masque about growing up, we may conveniently call *Comus* a *presentation*. Lady Alice was fifteen when she took the principal part, and there is an obvious propriety in having her tutor, Henry Lawes, present her, with her young brothers in attendance, to her father and mother:

> *Noble Lord, and Lady bright,*
> *I have brought ye new delight,*
> *Here behold so goodly grown*
> *Three fair branches of your own.* (965–8)

Milton himself was only twenty-six when he wrote *Comus*, and it is relevant so to remember when we attend to the Lady's opening soliloquy:

> This is the place, as well as I may guess,
> Whence even now the tumult of loud Mirth
> Was rife, and perfet in my list'ning ear,
> Yet naught but single darkness do I find. (200-3)

The perplexities of the wood are the perplexities of the waking adolescent imagination; the prospect of 'loud mirth' and the apprehension of 'single darkness'; the expectation of delight foiled by the fear of betrayal; a susceptibility to enchantments that subdue and daunt the imagination:

> A thousand fantasies
> Begin to throng into my memory
> Of calling shapes, and beckning shaddows dire
> And airy tongues that syllable mens names
> On Sands and Shores and desert Wildernesses. (204-8)

To foil the seductive voices that lure night-wanderers the Lady's resources are, naturally and rightly, moral in the rigorous admonitory sense:

> These thoughts may startle well, but not astound
> The vertuous mind, that ever walks attended
> By a strong siding champion Conscience. . . . (209-11)

These, and the lines that follow, make up the celestial panoply of puritanism, but they are also the bravely wielded moral weapons of youth and innocence. The young Lady looks eagerly for a sign that heaven has not abandoned her, and it comes in a form that the machinery of the masque can readily supply:[1]

> I did not err, there does a sable cloud
> Turn forth her silver lining on the night,
> And casts a gleam over this tufted Grove. (222-4)

[1] For refinements of this point see M. Nicolson, *A Reader's Guide to Milton*, p. 71, and C. H. Shattuck, 'Macready's *Comus*', *Milton Studies in Honor of H. F. Fletcher*, p. 131.

It is indeed a sign, and it fits felicitously enough into the masque's sequence of glimpses into the nature of grace—the Spirit assigned to be the lady's defence and guard, the sovran flower Haemony, the powers of Sabrina fair, and the last lines telling of heaven stooping to the aid of assailed virtue. But it is also about how the innocently lost and frightened young lady cheers herself up in the dark. The play's theological suggestions are in touch with youthful dismay and the recovery of spirits when a break in the clouds sets the Lady singing.

The experience of the brothers too has much to do with youthfulness. Neither their sword-arms nor their wisdom can avail unaided against Comus, though they are commended for their courage and 'bold emprise':

> Farr other arms and other weapons must
> Be those that quell the might of hellish charms;
> He with his bare wand can unthred thy joints
> And crumble all thy sinews. (611-14)

In the perspectives of the masque as a *presentation* it is clear that the moral vision and debating prowess of the Lady and her brothers is both warmly recommended and kept in its place. Their virtue is not the whole of virtue and it cannot be wholly efficacious; it needs divine and (in the masque) magical enhancement. But it is equally true that abstention and rigour are the doctrines proper to the wood. While in the wood we must not allow ourselves to be beguiled and seduced, or we shall dance with the deluded monsters in the dark. If for 'wood' we read 'while growing up' the masque confesses one relevance to life; but not the only one.

The other possibility is that the wood might signify life in general—the mortal condition. 'Bright aërial spirits' enjoy the calm and serene air, while men endure the 'smoke and stir', the 'dim darkness' and 'unhallowed air' of earth. The metaphors of light and darkness hold sway over this side of the masque:

> He that has light within his own clear breast
> May sit i'th center and enjoy bright day,
> But he that hides a dark soul and foul thoughts
> Benighted walks under the mid-day Sun. (380-3)

Milton writes in that Christian tradition that has been most responsive to Plato, to the Stoics, and to the Manicheans—stressing the sanctity of light and the remoteness of God from the world of the senses. Chastity for the Lady is a 'sun-clad power' that kindles the 'rapt spirits' to 'a flame of sacred vehemence'. Puritanism, Platonism and Manicheism have much in common, and ethical ideas derived from them are still lively enough to find their way unawares into discourse both more and less sophisticated. But once the intoxicated rabble is seen for what it is, there is no disputing the necessity for abstinence in the Lady's situation. And the rabble readily becomes an image of the soul 'clotted by contagion', of light imprisoned by darkness. Virtue must keep itself intact until it is recalled to the realms of light from which, like the Attendant Spirit, it first came.

I think that something is gained by temporarily setting apart, as I have done, the masque as a *presentation*—about growing up; and the masque as a neo-platonic allegory—about the survival of the spirit's purity in an alien sensual world. But other complications and resolutions remain to be traced.

To approach them, I would return to a consideration of the rhythmic and metaphoric eloquence of the masque—its way of casting spells. In response to the suggestion that the masque offers several kinds of verbal music, most of us would be quick to offer two: the sensual music of Comus's poetic dialect, and the moral music of the Elder Brother's.

'Sensual music' is a phrase borrowed from Yeats:

> The salmon-falls, the mackerel-crowded seas,
> Fish, flesh, or fowl, commend all summer long
> Whatever is begotten, born, and dies.
> Caught in that sensual music all neglect
> Monuments of unageing intellect.

The speech of Comus moves to a different rhythm but takes comparable delight in the prolific fecundity of the world; if to a different (Epicurean) end:

Wherefore did Nature pour her bounties forth
With such a full and unwithdrawing hand,
Covering the earth with odours, fruits and flocks,
Thronging the Seas with spawn innumerable,
But all to please and sate the curious taste? (709–13)

Comus's sensual music is made out of dance and turns back into dance:

The Sounds and Seas with all their finny drove
Now to the Moon in wavering Morrice move,
And on the Tawny Sands and Shelves
Trip the pert Fairies and the dapper Elves. (115–18)

The activity of the poetry is irresistible: 'Come, knit hands, and beat the ground/In a light fantastic round.' The words literally give place to dance, to 'The Measure', as the stage-direction has it, and Comus is in the first place disquieted not by rival words but by a rival measure:

I feel the different pace
Of som chaste footing near about this ground. (145–6)

And it is in part Milton's problem that he must find not merely arguments to displace the 'dear wit and gay rhetoric' of Comus, but rival rhythms and metaphors, energized from sources other than the prolific, spawning nature, that has become Comus's province.

The most fully orchestrated moral music is of the Elder Brother's performance, in a speech to which Milton responds with one of his most generous compliments to his own verse:

How charming is divine Philosophy!
Not harsh and crabbed as dull fools suppose,
But musical as is *Apollo's* lute,
And a perpetual feast of nectard sweets
Where no crude surfet reigns. (475–9)

Which declares well enough the ambition, if not the accomplishment, of Milton's more rigorous and puritanical rhetoric. It too is meant to 'charm', to enchant, to appease the senses. Milton spent a good part of his life looking for ways of making 'divine philosophy' as 'musical as is Apollo's lute'.[1]

The Elder Brother's speech, that occasions the Younger's delight, has much to deter us from Milton's endeavouring art:

> What was that snaky-headed *Gorgon shield*
> That wise *Minerva* wore, unconquerd Virgin,
> Wherewith she freez'd her foes to congeal'd stone,
> But rigid looks of Chaste austerity, (446–9)

But that is not, *pace* our reeling modern sensibility, the end of it. Where others may be daunted, Milton stays to admire:

> And noble grace that dashd brute violence
> With sudden adoration and blank awe? (450–51)

The word 'chasten' has almost faded from our vocabulary but here is an excuse to bring it back, associating virginity with a deterrent frigidity that arrests, spell-bound, the impulses of the seducer. But Milton speaks here through the boy, and the boy's vision is not in this respect vindicated.

The Lady is not a Gorgon, and Comus does not offer her brute violence. He casts a spell upon her that only Sabrina can dissolve. It is one of many warnings not to take the 'moral babble' as Milton's strongest voice. But then, neither is the 'sensual music'.

There is another, third kind, of verbal music, opening the masque and closing it, and heard from time to time within it. It is here, for instance, in the meditations of the Second Brother:

> But beauty like the fair Hesperian Tree
> Laden with blooming gold, had need the guard
> Of dragon watch with uninchanted eye,
> To save her blossoms and defend her fruit
> From the rash hand of bold Incontinence. (392–6)

---

[1] Keats in part shared the same ambition; see his comments on the *Comus* lines in his letter to George and Georgiana of Sunday 14 February 1819 (*Letters of John Keats*, ed. Buxton Forman (1947), p. 317).

It is the song that the Lady sings, and in Comus's response to it: the violet-embroidered vale, the nightingale, and the invocation:

> *So mayst thou be translated to the skies,*
> *And give resounding grace to all Heav'ns Harmonies.* (241–2)

This is the 'Divine inchanting ravishment', a Miltonic song quite distinct from the sensual music and the moral music, and yet related to both: a transfigured and sublimated sensuality. Listening to the Spirit epilogizing, we hear again the Hesperian music:

> To the Ocean now I fly,
> And those happy climes that ly
> Where day never shuts his eye,
> Up in the broad fields of the sky:
> There I suck the liquid air
> All amidst the Gardens fair
> Of *Hesperus*, and his daughters three
> That sing about the golden tree:
> Along the crisped shades and bowrs
> Revels the spruce and jocond Spring,
> The Graces and the rosie-bosomd Hours
> Thither all their bounties bring,
> There eternal Summer dwells,
> And West winds with musky wing
> About the cedar'n alleys fling
> *Nard* and *Cassia's* baumy smells. (975–90)

In Marlowe's *Hero and Leander* (line 786) the 'orchard of th' Hesperides' is an unequivocal symbol of sexual consummation and delight, but Milton's verse would perpetuate prolific joy in a Spring dance consonant with 'eternal Summer'. It is not strange that the Graces (born, Milton tells us in *L'Allegro* of 'lovely Venus' and 'Ivy-crowned Bacchus') should assume such dominion in the closing minutes of a masque of chastity, for they move among the blossoms and the fruits that the 'dragon watch with uninchanted eye' has defended from 'bold Incontinence'. Milton revisited his first draft of the poem to add to the epilogue some of the most etherial and satisfying of its lines for the printed edition of 1637—

the recollections of Spenser's Garden of Adonis, and the glimpse of
the wedding of Cupid and Psyche:

> Beds of *Hyacinth* and Roses
> Where young *Adonis* oft reposes,
> Waxing well of his deep wound
> In slumber soft, and on the ground
> Sadly sits th' *Assyrian* Queen;
> But far above in spangl'd sheen
> Celestial *Cupid* her fam'd son advanc't
> Holds his dear *Psyche* sweet intranc't
> After her wandring labours long,
> Till free consent the gods among
>   Make her his eternal Bride,
> And from her fair unspotted side
> Two blissful twins are to be born,
> Youth and Joy; so *Jove* hath sworn. (997–1010)

This is a yet rarer and more transcendent vision, intimating the
Divine Wedding, or ultimate ecstatic union of the soul with God.
It alights upon the mysterious but exquisite inter-relationship that
men and poets discover from time to time between sensual and
spiritual rapture. The masque does not, as E. M. W. Tillyard
supposed,[1] invite the girl to marry; but it is true that had the
occasion been a wedding and not a presentation, the liberated
senses might have found a less aereal retreat. It might then have
been clearer that the chaste maid can enjoy the 'sweet entrance-
ments' proper to the bridal state, because she has come safely
through the wood. As it is, the prospect is real but remote; it
belongs to the contemplative imagination. And the re-cast
epilogue marvellously sustains the poise of the whole device; for
if the spirit's vision allegorizes life, the Lady may expect to
marry; if it allegorizes death, the wedding will be transcendent
and divine.

The Lady, of course, does not owe her arrival merely to the
negative virtues she is called on to display. She owes it to the

---

[1] *Studies in Milton* (1951), p. 94; discussed by A. E. Dyson, 'The Interpretation
of Comus', *Essays and Studies* 1955.

E

Attendant Spirit, to the bright golden flower, to her brother's
swords, and to Sabrina. Reading the riddle (if riddle it be, but the
masque is often a riddling form) she owes it to her tutor, to those
who care for her, to the returning flow of natural life that Sabrina
represents when the girl is released from the seducer's spell,[1] and
she owes it to 'the Grace that Heaven lends', to moments of
miraculously strengthened resolution.

It would be inappropriate, however, to conclude with too
austere a stress upon the poet's exquisite moral design. The
pageant scene of Ludlow Town reminds us that the masque com-
memorates a civic as well as a domestic occasion; the company
meet 'in state' as the Earl assumes the Lord Presidency of Wales:

> And all this tract that fronts the falling Sun
> A noble Peer of mickle trust and power
> Has in his charge, with temperd awe to guide
> An old and haughty Nation proud in Arms (30–33)

What prerogatives of spacious and mature sovereignty Milton
attributes to Bridgewater! Poetry, spectacle, song and dance had a
continuing political efficacy inherited from the Elizabethan past;
Milton, in a tradition that Sidney understood, is holding a mirror
to the magistrate, and commends in order to command. But the
masque is an entertainment still:

> *The Scene changes, presenting* Ludlow *Town and the Presidents
> Castle, then com in Country-Dancers, after them the
> attendant Spirit, with the two Brothers and the Lady.* (956)

A dance, to a pageant background. As there are three rival verbal
musics, so there are three rival measures: the light fantastic of
Comus, the chaste footing of the lady; and now the Shropshire
country dancers. After the country dance with duck and nod,

---

[1] This I take to be Sabrina's principal significance; but her associations with
the River Severn, with Shropshire and the line of sovereignty from ancient
Troy (Locrine and Anchises) are quite as telling in the masque's political and
regional aspects.

Milton adroitly makes way for 'Other trippings to be trod'. The masque gives place to a ball.

In her valediction to the poem and its feverish critics, Rosemond Tuve finds that readers 'part company according to their philosophical postulates'; those who, like Milton, look with the eyes of the medieval realist or Platonist, and those nominalists and positivists who are unfitted by their presuppositions to acknowledge the two modes of reality upon which the power and eloquence of allegory depends.[1] It may be so. Convictions about the nature of reality may indeed restrict the range of our imaginings. But when the dance is under way, those who are reluctant to join it would do well to reflect, not upon the nature of reality, but on the processes by which *grace* has come to mean both 'charm, ease and refinement of movement' and 'the divine influence which operates in men to regenerate and sanctify, to inspire virtuous impulses, and to impart strength to endure trial and to resist temptation'.[2]

[1] *Images and Themes*, p. 159.

[2] Definitions adapted from the *O.E.D.* Shakespeare plays exquisitely with the word in *Love's Labour's Lost* (e.g. IV. iii. 67, V. ii. 786).

IV

Byron's Letters

JOHN D. JUMP

BYRON's letters constitute a brilliant portrait of their author.[1] But this fact does not account for the whole of their extraordinary interest. They provide glimpses of life in the England of his time and in the foreign countries through which he passed; they record his views on literature and politics and religion. In so far as they compose a bold and vivid self-portrait, however, they claim something of the status of a work of art. For they do not merely inform us; they coerce our imaginations as we read, until we seem almost to be in the presence of the living and speaking man.

He was a voluminous correspondent; and his voluminousness, both in prose and in verse, is no accidental characteristic. When we read his *Don Juan*, our sense of copiousness, of casual, uninhibited improvisation, is an important part of our total experience. The same is true when we turn to the letters. These are evidently the work of a writer who disposes easily and confidently of an abundance of matter and a wealth of words. What he offers us at any one moment is but a particular instance of his continuous, profuse, even careless productivity.

More than the mere bulk of his correspondence, the very texture of its prose draws attention to these qualities. Thomas

[1] Eight volumes contain most of Byron's published letters: the six volumes of *Letters and Journals,* edited by R. E. Prothero and published between 1898 and 1901, and the two volumes of *Lord Byron's Correspondence,* edited by John Murray and published in 1922. *Byron: A Self-Portrait,* edited by Peter Quennell and published in 1950, is a selection from these eight volumes, supplemented by some previously unprinted material. In the present paper, quotations from *Lord Byron's Correspondence* are ascribed to it in the text, the abbreviation *Correspondence* usually being employed. All other quotations from Byron's prose are taken from *Letters and Journals.*

Moore, who knew him well, informs us that Byron was in the habit of answering letters as soon as he received them; and Moore rightly suggests that this habit gave to his correspondence 'all the aptitude and freshness of replies in conversation' (*Prose and Verse* (1878), p. 421). From internal evidence alone, it is clear that, with few exceptions, Byron's are letters thrown off in haste. They are at the farthest remove from planned pronouncements. They give immediate utterance to whatever ideas or observations were suggested by his present circumstances and dominant feelings. So expressive are they of these feelings that they repeatedly come near to dramatic monologue. A good, but by no means exceptional, example is the letter to John Murray dated 14 March 1820.

Murray was Byron's publisher. Byron thought him a gentleman and 'a very good fellow' (29 January 1816), and regarded him as a friend, while never quite forgetting that theirs was after all a relationship between an aristocrat and a tradesman. He opens his letter in a friendly, informal, casual manner with a reference to a new poem, *The Prophecy of Dante*, the first four cantos of which he is sending:

DEAR MURRAY,—Enclosed is *Dante's Prophecy—Vision*—or what not.

This last phrase is a favourite of Byron's; again and again he cuts short a list with it, or with the similar 'and all that', and by so doing conveys a careless and slightly haughty refusal to specify further. In the present letter he continues with a bantering reference to Murray's 'Utican Senate' of die-hard literary advisers and indulges in a jibe at one of the senators, his friend Hobhouse, whose radical politics had recently landed him in gaol. He then directs his mockery on to himself. If the first instalment of *The Prophecy* is liked, he says, 'I will go on like Isaiah.' He exhorts Murray to take pains to see that the new volume is correctly printed.

He then turns to give news of himself and devotes the main part of his letter to an account of an accident which had happened

to him while driving outside Ravenna. A little premeditation
might have led him deliberately to postpone the climax of this
story. Instead, he rushes in, tells the worst at once, catalogues the
damage, and rounds off the sentence with a humorous comparison:

> Four days ago I was overturned in an open carriage between the
> river and a steep bank:—wheels dashed to pieces, slight bruises,
> narrow escape, and all that; but no harm done, though Coach-
> man, footman, horses, and vehicle, were all mixed together like
> Maccaroni.

It was natural to suppose that Murray would ask what caused the
spill.

> It was owing to bad driving, as I say; but the Coachman swears
> to a start on the part of the horses: we went against a post on the
> verge of a steep bank, and capsized.

Again, it was natural to suppose a question from Murray: How
did you come to be out driving at the place in question?

> I usually go out of the town in a carriage, and meet the saddle
> horses at the bridge: it was in going there that we boggled; but
> I got my ride, as usual, after the accident.

Having shown that the accident did not even suffice to deflect him
from his normal routine, Byron dismisses the topic with a laughing consideration of a theory favoured by the local people:

> They say here it was all owing to St. Antonio, of Padua (serious,
> I assure you), who does thirteen miracles a day, that worse did
> not come of it. I have no objection to this being his fourteenth
> in the four and twenty hours. He presides over overturns and
> all escapes therefrom, it seems: and they dedicate pictures, etc.,
> to him, as the Sailors once did to Neptune, after 'the high
> Roman Fashion'.
>
> Yours, in haste,
>
> B.

Byron's impetuosity here shows itself not only in the unrehearsed sequence of his thoughts but also in his not having paused to avoid such inelegances as 'a start on the part' and 'presides over overturns' and in his abrupt conclusion. His continuous awareness of his correspondent makes the passage read, as I have tried to suggest by interpolating Murray's supposed questions, almost like the utterances of one actually engaged in eager, friendly talk. The parenthesis in which he directly addresses Murray, 'serious, I assure you', is one of several phrases which give to the whole narrative a tone of careless, detached, quizzical humour; 'and all that' and 'it seems' also contribute to this effect. Byron does not wish Murray to take his spill too seriously; and his lightly mocking humour is more evident still in his initial description of the physical confusion and in his final references to St. Antonio.

His letters to Murray are not all as cheerful as this. On 20 September 1821, expressing the hope that certain of his papers will be edited for publication after his death, he writes:

The task will, of course, require delicacy; but that will not be wanting, if Moore and Hobhouse survive me, and, I may add, yourself; and that you may all three do so, is, I assure you, my very sincere wish. I am not sure that long life is desirable for one of my temper and constitutional depression of Spirits, which of course I suppress in society; but which breaks out when alone, and in my writings, in spite of myself. It has been deepened, perhaps, by some long past events (I do not allude to my marriage, etc.—on the contrary, *that* raised them by the persecution giving a fillip to my Spirits); but I call it constitutional, as I have reason to think it.

Here his gravity is momentarily relieved by the spurt of defiance on the subject of his marriage. Nevertheless, it dominates this passage and the greater part of the letter from which it comes.

Byron is equally in earnest,d an much more spirited, when, in his letter of 23 November 1820, he voices his hope that the Italians will not always remain subject to their Austrian oppressors. 'Of the state of things here,' he begins, 'it would be difficult and not very prudent to speak at large, the Huns opening all letters: I wonder if they can read them when they have opened them?' This question serves not only to give forcible expression to his indignation and contempt but also to remind him that Murray, to whom the letter is addressed, will not be its sole reader. The Austrian censor can be counted on to examine carefully anything the notorious English liberal sets down. He is a captive audience; and Byron in effect reduces Murray to eavesdropping as he proceeds to deliver his opinion of Austrian imperialism to the censor himself:

> I wonder if they can read them when they have opened them? if so, they may see, in my most legible hand, that I think them damned scoundrels and barbarians, their emperor a fool, and themselves more fools than he; all which they may send to Vienna, for anything I care. They have got themselves masters of the Papal police, and are bullying away; but some day or other they will pay for it all. It may not be very soon, because these unhappy Italians have no union nor consistency among themselves; but I suppose Providence will get tired of them at last, and show that God is not an Austrian.

Here, his robust and resentful denunciation of the oppressors, his menacing confidence that retribution will be exacted, and his sad acknowledgement of Italian unpreparedness are all serious enough. But they do not exclude the humorous assurance, from a man who knew well that his handwriting was difficult to read, that the unpalatable truths would be set down in his 'most legible hand'.

At other times, his scorn can be more particular, as when he condemns 'Johnny Keats's *piss a bed* poetry' (12 October 1820) or denounces William Sotheby as 'that wretched leper of literature—that Itch of Scribbling personified' (17 April 1818); and a similar, though less violent, anger could be provoked by Murray's dilatoriness during the later years of their correspondence, a dilatoriness which may have been motivated in part by a reluctance to go on publishing the subversive *Don Juan* and which eventually helped to drive Byron to another publisher. But his ferocity is decidedly jocular when he rounds off his letter of 25 May 1821 with the words:

Yours, in haste and hatred, you scrubby correspondent!
B.

In fact, his anger, his gravity, and his earnestness of every kind keep turning to humour as he writes. We can watch this happen, and then see Byron deliberately reverse the tendency, in his affectionate letter of 8 March 1822 to the closest of his friends, the poet Tom Moore. In this, he refers to the current attacks on himself for writing and on Murray for publishing the allegedly blasphemous *Cain* and to his resultant decision to continue one of Murray's authors after all. He goes on:

I really feel ashamed of having bored you so frequently and fully of late. But what could I do? You are a friend—an absent one, alas!—and as I trust no one more, I trouble you in proportion.

This war of 'Church and State' has astonished me more than it disturbs; for I really thought *Cain* a speculative and hardy, but still a harmless, production. As I said before, I am really a great admirer of tangible religion; and am breeding one of my daughters a Catholic, that she may have her hands full. It is by far the most elegant worship, hardly excepting the Greek mythology. What with incense, pictures, statues, altars, shrines, relics, and the real presence, confession, absolution,—there is something sensible to grasp at. Besides, it leaves no possibility of doubt; for those who swallow their Deity, really and truly, in transubstantiation, can hardly find any thing else otherwise than easy of digestion.

I am afraid that this sounds flippant, but I don't mean it to be so; only my turn of mind is so given to taking things in the absurd point of view, that it breaks out in spite of me every now and then. Still, I do assure you that I am a very good Christian. Whether you will believe me in this, I do not know; but I trust you will take my word for being
Very truly and affectionately yours, etc.

Moore and Byron had a very warm regard for each other. Byron thought Moore 'the best-hearted, the only *hearted* being I ever encountered' ('Journal', 10 December 1813) and got on with him the more easily because he was no mere scribbler but a man of the world. Shortly after Byron's death, Moore composed '"The Living Dog" and "The Dead Lion"', surely our classical protest by an admirer of a great man against the posthumous defilement of his reputation by the issuing of ungenerous and disparaging 'Reminiscences'. For Moore had not only the sentimental vein which yielded 'The Minstrel Boy', ' 'Tis the Last Rose of Summer', 'The Harp that Once through Tara's Halls', and 'Believe Me, If All those Endearing Young Charms' but also a lively satirical wit. So had Byron, and he gives exuberant expression to it in his letter of 24 December 1816 to Moore. In this, he tells a story he has just heard in Milan about a young British junior officer who had been parted from his Italian mistress by the outbreak of war between England and France in 1793; and who, when the first fall of Napoleon temporarily restored peace in 1814, returned as a colonel to claim her. Byron does not fail to exploit the fact that the officer was, like Moore, an Irishman.

Six-and-twenty years ago, Col. [Fitzgerald], then an ensign, being in Italy, fell in love with the Marchesa [Castiglione], and she with him. The lady must be, at least, twenty years his senior. The war broke out; he returned to England, to serve— not his country, for that's Ireland—but England, which is a different thing; and *she*—heaven knows what she did. In the year 1814, the first annunciation of the Definitive Treaty of Peace (and tyranny) was developed to the astonished Milanese by the arrival of Col. [Fitzgerald], who, flinging himself full length at the feet of Mad. [Castiglione], murmured forth, in half-forgotten Irish Italian, eternal vows of indelible constancy. The lady screamed, and exclaimed, 'Who are you?' The Colonel cried, 'What! don't you know me? I am so and so', etc., etc., etc.; till, at length, the Marchesa, mounting from reminiscence to reminiscence, through the lovers of the intermediate twenty-five years, arrived at last at the recollection of her *povero* sub-lieutenant. She then said, 'Was there ever such virtue?' (that was her very word) and, being now a widow, gave him apartments in her palace, reinstated him in all the rights of wrong, and held him up to the admiring world as a miracle of incontinent fidelity, and the unshaken Abdiel of absence.

Here, as often elsewhere, Byron scoffs at 'sentimental and sensibilitous' (29 June 1811) persons. The romantic lover murmurs forth 'eternal vows of indelible constancy'; Byron observes that he does so in 'half-forgotten Irish Italian'. When the Marchesa peers back into her love-life, the structure of Byron's sentence comically reflects the stages by which she mounts to the recollection of her suitor. Her reunion with him terminates the little satirical farce; and it is the irony of a gay and resourceful raconteur which plays upon her praise of his 'virtue', her reinstatement of him 'in all the rights of wrong', her upholding him 'as a miracle of incontinent fidelity', and her final comparison of him with the loyal seraph in *Paradise Lost*. A similarly lightly mocking treatment of the cant of sensibility characterizes Byron's later presentation of Julia's love-affair in Canto I of *Don Juan*.

Moore's cheerful sociability made him a very suitable recipient for Byron's high-spirited description, in his letter of 31 October 1815, of a party at which 'all was hiccup and happiness for the last hour or so'. Byron, who was well aware of the comic possibilities of the catalogue, whether in verse or in prose, here lists the eight stages of conviviality:

Like other parties of the kind, it was first silent, then talky, then argumentative, then disputatious, then unintelligible, then altogethery, then inarticulate, and then drunk. When we had reached the last step of this glorious ladder, it was difficult to get down again without stumbling; and, to crown all, Kinnaird and I had to conduct Sheridan down a damned corkscrew staircase, which had certainly been constructed before the discovery of fermented liquors, and to which no legs, however crooked, could possibly accommodate themselves. We deposited him safe at home, where his man, evidently used to the business, waited to receive him in the hall.

After the polysyllabic labels applied to the five previous stages—'altogethery' being a particularly apt coinage—the monosyllable 'drunk' ends the list with a conclusive thud. The whole passage is representative in its flexibility, vigour, and raciness of language.

Douglas Kinnaird, who helped to take home the convivial author of *The School for Scandal*, was at this time a regular associate of Byron's and later became his business adviser, his 'trusty and trust-worthy trustee and banker, and crown and sheet-anchor' (13 December 1823). The poet's decision to place his fortune, as well as his life, at the service of the Greek national movement, made him continue in close touch with Kinnaird throughout his last year. In general, correspondents knew a somewhat more sober Byron during this period, and his letters to Kinnaird and others at the time of the Greek enterprise are notably judicious, practical, and resolute. Another firm friend, an older and more intimate one than Kinnaird, was John Cam Hobhouse, with whom Byron had embarked upon his Mediterranean tour in 1809. Hobhouse was a loyal, sensible, and candid ally: 'a cynic after my own heart' (*Correspondence*, 7 May 1813), said Byron. He did not hesitate to tell Byron his faults, and Byron frequently made him the butt of affectionate laughter. While their relationship was not free from friction, each man retained a sincere respect for the other's independence. On this point, the evidence of the letters is clear. 'After all,' wrote Byron, when he and Hobhouse had parted in 1810, before the end of his Mediterranean tour, 'I do love thee, Hobby, thou hast so many good qualities, and so many bad ones, it is impossible to live with thee or without thee' (*Correspondence*, 23 August 1810). The greater part of Byron's liveliest and most intimate correspondence with male friends seems to have been addressed to Hobhouse, Kinnaird, Murray and Moore.

In general, female correspondents came off less well. Byron insisted that 'Lovers . . . never can be friends' (10 November

1822), and his letters to his lovers suffered accordingly. No one can say for certain whether his half-sister Augusta was his lover or not; if she was, their congenital relationship must have sustained a friendship which sexual love would otherwise have overthrown. At all events, Augusta was one of the two women who received excellent letters from him during his adult years.

He had no very high opinion of her abilities. But she was good-natured, affectionate, and a Byron. His letters to her tend to be simple, relaxed, gossipy, playful. During the autumn of 1822, there was an extraordinary rainfall in the part of Italy where he was living. On 7 November, he sent Augusta a report of the facts with an embroidery of fanciful and absurd inventions. This account illustrates the remarkable mobility of his temperament. He feels surprise and bewilderment at the violence of the deluge and the devastation caused by it; but his irony asserts itself when he records that his own household, with the 'lower floor afloat', enjoyed a 'comfortable view of the whole landscape under water, and people screaming out of their garret windows'; after noting, with the additional emphasis given by underlining, that there were '*two bridges* swept down', he provides a delightful and ludicrous description of the looting of neighbouring shops by the turbulent elements, 'which marched away with a quantity of shoes, several Perukes, and Gingerbread in all its branches'; finally, he expresses simple astonishment at the suddenness and volume of the flood and at the drowning of a child 'a few yards from its own door'.

An extravagant humour dominates the rest of the letter:

Well, after all this comes a preaching Friar and says that the day of Judgement will take place positively on the *4th* with all kinds of tempest and what not, in consequence of which the whole City (except some impious Scoffers) sent him presents to avert the wrath of Heaven by his prayers, and even the *public authorities* had warned the Captains of Ships, who, to mend the matter, almost all bought *new Cables* and anchors by way of weathering the Gale.

But the fourth turned out a very fine day. All those who had paid their money are excessively angry, and insist either upon having the day of judgement or their cash again. But the

Friar's device seems to be 'no money to be returned,' and he says that he merely made a mistake in the time, for the day of Judgement will certainly come for all that, either here or in some other part of Italy.

This has a little pacified the expectants. You will think this a fiction. Enquire further then. The populace actually used to kiss the fellow's feet in the streets.

Byron's other most-favoured female correspondent was Lady Melbourne, an older woman who was his honorary 'aunt' during his years of fame in England. At the period when he was writing to her regularly, he set down in his journal-entry for 24 November 1813:

To Lady Melbourne I write with most pleasure—and her answers, so sensible, so *tactique*—I never met with half her talent. If she had been a few years younger, what a fool she would have made of me, had she thought it worth her while,— and I should have lost a valuable and most agreeable *friend*.

On 16 March 1818, he expressed himself similarly in a letter to Moore: 'She was my greatest *friend*, of the feminine gender:— when I say "friend," I mean *not* mistress, for that's the antipode.' His letters to her, as printed in *Lord Byron's Correspondence*, are more sophisticated in tone and characterized by a sharper curiosity regarding human behaviour than are his letters to Augusta. On 5 September 1813, for example, he records an impression of the young woman who later became his wife:

She seems to have been spoiled—not as children usually are—but systematically Clarissa Harlowed into an awkward kind of correctness, with a dependence upon her own infallibility which will or may lead her into some egregious blunder. I don't mean the usual error of young gentlewomen, but she will find exactly what she wants, and then discover that it is much more dignified than entertaining.

The compact phrases 'systematically Clarissa Harlowed' and

'more dignified than entertaining' accurately define the character, and plausibly predict the future, of the precise, formal, and rather complacent Annabella Milbanke. She is also the subject of candid investigation on 4, 6, and 13 November 1814, shortly before their marriage.

While visiting an absurd acquaintance, James Wedderburn Webster, Byron found himself involved in an intrigue reminiscent of Restoration comedy. Before the plot became really complicated, he wrote to Lady Melbourne on 21 September 1813:

W[ebster] don't want sense, nor good nature, but both are occasionally obscured by his suspicions, and absurdities of all descriptions; he is passionately fond of having his wife admired, and at the same time jealous to jaundice of everything and everybody. I have hit upon the medium of praising her to him perpetually behind her back, and never looking at her before his face; as for her, I believe she is disposed to be very faithful, and I don't think anyone now here is inclined to put her to the test. W[ebster] himself is, with all his jealousy and admiration, a little tired; he has been lately at Newstead,[1] and wants to go again. I suspected this sudden *penchant*, and soon discovered that a foolish nymph of the Abbey, about whom fortunately I care not, was the attraction. Now if I wanted to make mischief I could extract much good perplexity from a proper management of such events; but I am grown so good, or so indolent, that I shall not avail myself of so pleasant an opportunity of tormenting mine host, though he deserves it for poaching. I believe he has hitherto been unsuccessful, or rather it is too astonishing to be believed.

Here, asides and afterthoughts—'about whom fortunately I care not', 'or so indolent', 'though he deserves it for poaching', 'or rather it is too astonishing to be believed'—develop the tone of polite, detached amusement established by the antithetical constructions with which the passage opens. We are reminded of Byron's tellingly qualified praise of the Roman Catholic as 'by far the most elegant worship, *hardly excepting the Greek mythology*'. But he has more to say about the uxorious Webster:

[1] Newstead Abbey, Byron's house.

He proposed to me, with great gravity, to carry him over there [that is, to Newstead and the nymph], and I replied with equal candour, that *he* might set out when he pleased, but that I should remain here to take care of his household in the interim —a proposition which I thought very much to the purpose, but which did not seem at all to his satisfaction. By way of opiate he preached me a sermon on his wife's good qualities, concluding by an assertion that in all moral and mortal qualities, she was very like 'Christ! ! !' I think the Virgin Mary would have been a more appropriate typification; but it was the first comparison of the kind I ever heard, and made me laugh till he was angry, and then I got out of humour too, which pacified him, and shortened the panegyric.

This is the narrative of one who knows that he is addressing an alert, experienced, sympathetic, and worldly-wise woman. The egregious Webster emerges very clearly from it.

At a later stage, when it was conceivable that the two men might fight a duel about Webster's wife, Byron took humorous consolation in the thought that his death in such circumstances 'would be so *dramatic* a conclusion; all the sex would be enamoured of my memory, all the wits would have their jests, and the moralists their sermon. C[aroline Lamb] would go wild with *grief* that *it did not happen about her*' (*Correspondence*, 25 November 1813).

Such is the self-portrait which these letters compose. They show Byron as impulsive, even reckless; quick to feel resentment and aggressive in his anger. At times, as he acknowledges, he is subject to feelings of profound despondency. But these afflict him more in solitude than in society; so they are more prominent in his poetry and his journals than in his letters, letter-writing being inevitably in some degree a social activity. It was particularly so with him, his letters being scribbled rapidly and spontaneously with the image of each correspondent vividly present to his mind. Wit and humour are never long absent; and there is no denying the truth of his insistence that such friends as Moore knew him not as a 'misanthropical and gloomy gentleman . . . but [as] a facetious companion, well to do with those with whom I am intimate, and as loquacious and laughing as if I were a much cleverer fellow' (10 March 1817). It amuses him to tell Moore of a young American who visited him, expecting 'to meet a misanthropical gentleman, in wolf-skin breeches, and answering in fierce monosyllables' (5 July 1821). He is friendly, exuberant, derisive, voluble, pugnacious, outspoken, and genial. These qualities receive highly colloquial and even dramatic expression in his impatient retort of 6 April 1819 to Murray's suggestion that he should give up seven or eight years to composing a great literary work:

> So you and Mr. Foscolo, etc., want me to undertake what you call a 'great work?' an Epic poem, I suppose, or some such pyramid. I'll try no such thing; I hate tasks. And then 'seven or eight years!' God send us all well this day three months, let alone years. If one's years can't be better employed than in sweating poesy, a man had better be a ditcher. And works, too!—is *Childe Harold* nothing? You have so many '*divine*' poems, is it nothing to have written a *Human* one? without any of your worn-out machinery. Why, man, I could have spun the thoughts of the four cantos of that poem into twenty, had I wanted to book-make, and its passion into as many modern tragedies. Since you want *length*, you shall have enough of *Juan*, for I'll make 50 cantos.[1]

He always felt some scorn for the sedentary trade to which he devoted so much of his life. He was ill at ease in the company of all but a very few of his fellow-writers: 'I never know what to say to them after I have praised their last publication' ('Detached Thoughts', 53). He preferred men of fashion, and he very much preferred men of action. It was as a man of action, translating his faith in freedom and hatred of despotism into deeds, that he lived his last months in a Greece fighting for independence.

It is a fascinating personality that we meet in these letters, and the letters are intrinsically important mainly because they enable us to meet it. But they have an importance of another kind for

---

[1] This explosion staggered Murray: 'I never read a more powerful Letter in my life' (*Letters and Journals*, iv. 286).

F

those interested in Byron's poetry. Until 1818, this must indeed have seemed to be the work of a 'misanthropical and gloomy gentleman'. Then, in *Beppo, Don Juan*, and *The Vision of Judgment*, Byron transcended the childish and theatrical romanticism of so much of his earlier verse and produced the great anti-romantic and disconcertingly truthful serio-comic poetry of his maturity. Dominating this, there stands the literary personality we have been meeting in the letters. The interesting thing is that this personality was present in Byron's letters long before 1818, the date when it began effectively to invade his verse. Of the longer passages that I have quoted, four—the verdict on Annabella Milbanke, the portrait of Wedderburn Webster, the description of the drinking-party, and the narrative of Colonel Fitzgerald's belated reunion with his mistress—were written before 1818; and these offer already a kind of prose that is the equivalent of what we value in *Don Juan*. In short, Byron's letters supply convincing evidence that the powers which he was successfully mobilizing for the first time as a poet during his last half-dozen years were powers which he had long possessed but which romantic inhibitions had hitherto prevented him from exploiting fully in verse.

Among these was his power of alert and shrewd observation of his fellow men and women. To Lady Melbourne, he wrote: 'anything that confirms, or extends one's observations on life and character delights me' (*Correspondence*, 1 October 1813). So we should not be surprised to find him attending a public execution and noting not only the behaviour of the condemned persons but also his own reaction to the spectacle (30 May 1817); or reporting with the keenest interest and in considerable detail the shooting, and the subsequent death after being carried indoors, of the military commandant in Ravenna (9 December 1820). His letters contain many lively portraits of friends and acquaintances. As well as the sharp sketches of Annabella Milbanke and Wedderburn Webster, there are, for example, the passages concerned with his literary relative, R. C. Dallas (3 October 1810); his valet, William Fletcher (14 January 1811); Madame de Staël (*Correspondence*, 8 August 1813 and 8 January 1814); the Italian poet, Pindemonte (4 June 1817); the fantastic Dr. Polidori (24 January 1817, 17 June

1817); Porson, the classical scholar (20 February 1818); John Hanson, Byron's solicitor (*Correspondence*, 11 November 1818); Angelina, one of his Venetian mistresses (18 May 1819); Allegra, his illegitimate daughter (31 March 1820); Maria Edgeworth's father (4 November 1820); Byron's dead friend, C. S. Matthews (19 November 1820); and the Hunts and Shelley (*passim*).

But the fullest and most revealing of his epistolary portraits is that of his Venetian mistress, Margarita Cogni, which he wrote on 1 August 1819 in response to a request from Murray. This is a fascinatingly detailed character-study, more than five times as long as the few paragraphs which must suffice to represent it here. Byron speaks of Margarita's ascendancy over him:

> The reasons of this were, firstly, her person—very dark, tall, the Venetian face, very fine black eyes—and certain other qualities which need not be mentioned. She was two and twenty years old, and, never having had children, had not spoilt her figure ... She was, besides, a thorough Venetian in her dialect, in her thoughts, in her countenance, in every thing, with all their naïveté and Pantaloon humour. Besides, she could neither read nor write, and could not plague me with letters,—except twice that she paid sixpence to a public scribe, under the piazza, to make a letter for her, upon some occasion, when I was ill and could not see her. In other respects she was somewhat fierce and *prepotente*, that is, overbearing, and used to walk in whenever it suited her, with no very great regard to time, place, nor persons; and if she found any women in her way, she knocked them down. . . .
>
> Madame Benzone . . . took her under her protection, and then her head turned. She was always in extremes, either crying or laughing; and so fierce when angered, that she was the terror of men, women, and children—for she had the strength of an Amazon, with the temper of Medea. She was a fine animal, but quite untameable. *I* was the only person that could at all keep her in any order, and when she saw me really angry (which they tell me is rather a savage sight), she subsided. But she had a thousand fooleries: in her *fazziolo*, the dress of the lower orders, she looked beautiful; but, alas! she longed for a hat and feathers, and all I could say or do (and I said much) could not prevent this

travestie. I put the first into the fire; but I got tired of burning them, before she did of buying them, so that she made herself a figure—for they did not at all become her. . . .

In the mean time, she beat the women and stopped my letters. I found her one day pondering over one: she used to try to find out by their shape whether they were feminine or no; and she used to lament her ignorance, and actually studied her Alphabet, on purpose (as she declared) to open all letters addressed to me and read their contents.

I must not omit to do justice to her housekeeping qualities: after she came into my house as *donna di governo*, the expences were reduced to less than half, and every body did their duty better—the apartments were kept in order, and every thing and every body else, except herself. . . .

I forgot to mention that she was very devout, and would cross herself if she heard the prayer-time strike—sometimes when that ceremony did not appear to be much in unison with what she was then about.

Animating the whole of this description, and inspiring its author's choice of anecdotes, is something which is evident from the beginning in Byron's work both in prose and in verse: his ready responsiveness to every manifestation of instinctive energy. As he wrote in his journal on 23 November 1813, 'I like energy—even animal energy—of all kinds'.

But in its lively appreciation of human idiosyncrasy the passage is strikingly different from anything that we should expect to find in the poetry Byron published before 1818. In the letters of those earlier years, we have glimpses of Dallas, Fletcher, Madame de Staël, Annabella Milbanke, Wedderburn Webster, Pindemonte, and Polidori; in the verse of the same period we encounter only such attitudinizing dummies as Childe Harold, Conrad the Corsair, and Manfred—dummies capable of provoking the suspicion that their creator knew about the human race only from hearsay. From 1818 onwards, however, Byron's verse as well as his prose testifies to his eager and perceptive observation of life. He found it possible to admit to *Don Juan* and *The Vision of Judgment* the humour, the satire, and above all the realism, the fidelity to life as he had really experienced it, of which his correspondents had long known him capable but for which he had found little or no place in his rather extensive romantic juvenilia.

These poems in *ottava rima* are his finest achievements as an artist. They express a zest for life which is conditioned but not inhibited by a sober sense of what life really is. In their degree, his letters express the same thing, as do his journals; and they express it, powerfully and unforgettably, by projecting upon our imaginations the living and speaking presence of their author.

V

A Background for 'Empedocles on Etna'

KENNETH ALLOTT

TEN years ago an American scholar remarked of Matthew Arnold's 'Empedocles on Etna' that 'no other Victorian poem of such demonstrable stature has been so neglected,'[1] by which he meant presumably that it had not at that time been made the subject of much interpretation by academic critics. In this special and professional sense of the word 'neglected' the remark is no longer true. Since 1960 there has been a flood of interpretative criticism of Arnold's poetry, mostly by American critics, and 'Empedocles on Etna' has received its full share of attention. The present essay does not seek to discuss these interpretations or to add to their number. Instead it proposes to inquire what light is shed on 'Empedocles on Etna' if we ask in what relation it stands to Arnold's earlier and later poems and why at this point in his career he chose Empedocles as a poetic subject.

I

In his poem 'Stanzas from the Grande Charteuse', which was first published in 1855 but had probably been on the stocks for several years,[2] Arnold confessed that

> . . . rigorous teachers seized my youth,
> And prun'd its faith and quench'd its fire,
> Show'd me the pale cold star of Truth,
> There bade me gaze, and there aspire.[3]

---

[1] 'Arnold's "Empedocles on Etna"', *Victorian Studies* i (June 1958), p. 311.

[2] It recalls a honeymoon visit to the monastery in September 1851.

[3] The text is from *Fraser's Magazine* (April 1855). The 1867 readings 'purged its faith, and trimm'd its fire' and 'high, white star of Truth' in *New Poems* are less candid.

There has been speculation on the names of the 'rigorous teachers' intended to be supplied, but the shortest list would have to make room for Goethe, Senancour, Lucretius, Epictetus and Spinoza, who are among the men with whose writings Arnold struggled most manfully in the 1840s in his pursuit of that 'intellectual deliverance' described by him in his inaugural lecture as Professor of Poetry at Oxford in 1857 as 'the peculiar demand of those ages which are called modern'.[1] Devotion to 'the pale cold star of Truth' was never to be denied by Arnold, but here his confession is also a complaint: the 'genuine feelings of unrest, loneliness and dissatisfaction' which T. S. Eliot finds in the best poems, and which the younger Arnold was too honest a poet to suppress, indicate that any feeling of joyful emancipation produced by this necessary 'intellectual deliverance' was quickly qualified by a sense of loss that grew sharper with the passing of time. 'Forlorn', the epithet chosen by Keats to describe the return to reality in the 'Ode to a Nightingale', is Arnold's epithet in 'Stanzas from the Grande Chartreuse' as he contemplates 'la poussière de toutes les croyances tombées'—

> Wandering between two worlds, one dead
> The other powerless to be born,
> With nowhere yet to rest my head,
> Like these, on earth I wait forlorn . . .

and he begs forgiveness of his 'masters of the mind' if his melancholy seems to compromise their 'truth'. It has to be grasped that Arnold's scepticism was always, except perhaps at the very outset, reluctant. In *Every Man His Own Poet or the Inspired Singer's Recipe Book* (1872) the author (who called himself 'a Newdigate Prizeman' and who was in fact W. H. Mallock) begins his recipe 'How to write a poem like Mr. Matthew Arnold' with the injunction 'Take one soulfull of *involuntary* unbelief' (my italics) and goes on to stress that the tonality of the poetry, for all Arnold's efforts at *Tüchtigkeit*, is one of melancholy and nostalgic regret.

---

[1] *Complete Prose Works*, ed. R. H. Super, i (1960), p. 19. Cited below as *Prose Works*.

The temper of Arnold's mind remained fundamentally religious because, in spite of his youthful revolt against the narrowness and strictness of his upbringing at Rugby and Fox How, and in spite of his knowledge that his father thought him to be both too independent and too indolent, his boyhood, taken as a whole, was a singularly secure and happy one. It is now customary to attribute conflict to an unhappy childhood, but from a psychological viewpoint Arnold's conflicts arose from his inability to feel that an 'intellectual deliverance' that cut him off from full communion with the warmth and happiness of the family circle could be anything but culpably unfilial.

Yet the 'intellectual deliverance' had begun with Dr. Arnold, who inculcated open-mindedness and a spirit of inquiry on his sons and daughters and his favourite sixth-formers at Rugby in the firm belief that devotion to truth and devotion to Christianity could not be at odds. Matthew saw his father, for all the latter's severity and imaginative limitations (he was shocked by Byron, troubled by Goethe's *Faust*), as an intellectual liberator. Consequently, when he went up to Balliol in 1841 and the beliefs that were never shaken for Dr. Arnold began to grow unreal, he continued to feel, as his training had taught him to feel, that an unavoidable duty was laid on every individual 'to get breast to breast with reality'.[1] It was a duty not to be postponed. There could be no luxuriating in poetic sensation, no Tennysonian 'dawdling' with the world's 'painted shell'.[2] The problem of man's place in the sum of things became pressing when the original props of belief were knocked away. Mrs. Humphry Ward believed that George Sand's novels opened 'a world of artistic beauty and joy'[3] to Matthew and his younger brother Tom at Oxford, but the recently published 'Equator Letters' composed by Tom Arnold on his voyage to New Zealand (November 1847–January 1848)[4]

---

[1] *The Letters of Matthew Arnold to A. H. Clough*, ed. H. F. Lowry (1932), p. 86. Cited below as 'Lowry'.

[2] Lowry, p. 63.

[3] *A Writer's Recollections* (1918), p. 12.

[4] *New Zealand Letters of Thomas Arnold the Younger*, ed. J. Bertram (1966), pp. 207–19.

show that this is a simplification of the truth. Tom Arnold's interest in George Sand was aroused almost exclusively by her passionate cry against social injustice. Matthew's enthusiasm for the French novelist was more aesthetic, but it is clear that he read her primarily, as he read *Wilhelm Meister* (in Carlyle's translation), for the artistic presentation of a 'large, liberal view of human life'.[1] There were shifts of emphasis in mental stance between 1843 and 1847, but broadly speaking the 'rigorous teachers' were wrestled with by Arnold as an undergraduate, as a young Fellow of Oriel, and later as Lord Lansdowne's private secretary in London, in an attempt to furnish himself with the elements of a creed that would not affront the critical intellect by its supernaturalism but would nevertheless allow him to salvage at least the possibility of reverence from the wreckage of the orthodox beliefs in which he had been reared. He studied Goethe or Lucretius or the *Bhagavad Gita* for enlightenment, but also, obscurely, to obtain spiritual reassurance, and this second purpose grew more explicit as time went on.

So much can be deciphered of the steady reality behind the mask of the light-hearted dandy with which Arnold faced the world at Oxford or in Mayfair. He appeared to be a man who could always be distracted from his books by a day's fishing or an evening's whist. He was ready to talk absurdities and many of his friends thought him frivolous. 'I laugh too much and they make one's laughter mean too much,' he wrote to J. D. Coleridge in 1844.[2] How successful a mask it was we know because some of his brothers and sisters, not to mention these friends, were surprised by the earnestness and melancholy of his first collection of verse, *The Strayed Reveller, and Other Poems*, in 1849. 'The common assumption that he wholly lacked a capacity for philosophical thinking is mistaken,' claims a recent critic. 'It might be said rather that he could not be a dutiful schoolman, discovering the mind's happiness within the boundaries set upon thought by any single school or sect.'[3] The concealed intellectual effort expended

---

[1] 'Emerson', *Discourses in America* (1896 edn.), p. 143.

[2] *Life and Correspondence of John Duke Coleridge*, ed. E. H. Coleridge (1904), i, p. 145.

[3] Warren D. Anderson, *Matthew Arnold and the Classical Tradition* (1965), p. 134.

by Arnold in the 1840s was considerable and the small degree of success achieved in certain directions disheartening. We hear him saying wrily to Clough at the end of 1847 or early in 1848 '... you may often hear my sinews cracking under the effort to unite matter',[1] and to his sister Jane in an undated letter belonging to the summer of 1849 he explains self-deprecatingly that his poems are fragmentary and 'stagger weakly and are at their wits' end' because 'I am fragments'.[2] It was not for want of trying that he was forced to this honest admission.

A few years later Arnold wondered aloud if he had not deformed his nature and perverted his poetic gift by the earnestness with which behind his monocle and languid manner he had sought to construct a philosophy of life in the decade following his father's death. 'I feel immensely—more and more clearly—what I *want*—what I have (I believe) lost and choked by my treatment of myself and the studies to which I have addicted myself,' he admitted to Clough in May 1853. 'But what ought I to have done in preference to what I have done? there is the question.'[3]

It is, of course, an unanswerable question. To Arnold in the 1840s it seemed that there was only one course open, and, knowing what we know now of his temperament and background, it is hard to see how he could have acted otherwise. He recognized that he must 'begin with an Idea of the world in order not to be prevailed over by the world's multitudinousness',[4] but how was an adequate idea of this sort to be gained? He puzzled himself with metaphysics and was irritated by the arid abstractions of German idealism into some respect for the common sense of Locke, who, however, lacked 'the positive and vivifying atmosphere of Spinoza'.[5] Spinoza's serenity was vivifying, but his arguments against final causes were dismissed as casuistical. In weaker

[1] Lowry, p. 65.

[2] *Unpublished Letters of Matthew Arnold*, ed. A. Whitridge (1923), p. 18. The editor speculatively dates the letter '1853', but the reference to the siege of Rome by the French establishes the correct date.

[3] Lowry, p. 136.

[4] Lowry, p. 97.

[5] Lowry, p. 117.

moments he feared that 'We read to avoid the labour of an inward survey and arrangement—and are but heaping up more to be surveyed and arranged in some inevitable future'.[1] By September 1849 he had decided that his 'one natural craving' was 'not for profound thoughts, mighty spiritual workings, etc., etc., but a distinct seeing of my way as far as my own nature is concerned...'[2] He could not have settled for so much less than 'the truth, the whole truth, and nothing but the truth' if he had not by then convinced himself laboriously that metaphysical questions receive dusty answers:

> Hither and thither spins
> The wind-borne, mirroring soul,
> A thousand glimpses wins,
> And never sees a whole;
> Looks once, and drives elsewhere, and leaves its last employ.[3]

The bearing of this early chapter of Arnold's intellectual history on his poetic development has often been overlooked or insufficiently allowed for. He was a youth of nineteen when his father died suddenly of heart-disease at Rugby in June 1842. Elder sons, says Newman in *Loss and Gain*, 'should their father die prematurely, are suddenly ripened into manhood, when they are almost boys'.[4] The 'first sorrow, which is childhood's grave'[5] completely changed the circumstances of the Arnold family, made Matthew its titular head, and gave to his intellectual explorations a new and more personal urgency. The loss of his father freed him from an antagonism that was never more than a son's need not to be completely overshadowed, but it also gave him the private grief that now it was too late to justify himself. He 'plunged very deeply in the years following his father's death', wrote his brother Tom, 'in the vast sea of Goethe's art and Spinoza's mysticism'.[6] Through

---

[1] Unpublished note in the Yale MS.

[2] Lowry, p. 110.

[3] 'Empedocles on Etna' I. ii. 82–6.

[4] Part I, Chapter 18.

[5] The phrase is from Arnold's Newdigate prize-poem *Cromwell* (1843).

[6] *Manchester Guardian*, 18 May 1888.

Goethe read as a sage rather than as a poet, he came to Spinoza. From both men he drew the lesson of the inadequacy of Romantic self-assertion and the necessity of submission to the universal order. Epictetus confirmed the lesson and also taught him that some questions 'are perhaps incomprehensible to the human mind' and that it is enough 'to know the nature of good and evil' and 'not to trouble ourselves about the things above us'.[1]

Arnold's assent to the eclectic variety of Stoic ethics preached to Pausanias as practical wisdom in the second scene of 'Empedocles on Etna' was always more intellectual than emotional while he was still capable of writing poetry. 'Close thy *Byron*; open thy *Goethe*', Carlyle had trumpeted in *Sartor Resartus*, but Arnold remained in two minds. He opened his Goethe obediently, but he could not suppress a sneaking admiration for Byron's defiant energy or pretend that he had no sympathy for the discontented aspiration of Senancour's Obermann. In 'Mycerinus', which is probably in conception one of Arnold's earliest pieces (apart from juvenilia and prize-poems), there is no submission: the universal order that decrees an early death for a good man is seen as a 'tyrannous necessity'. (It is difficult not to take the poem as an expression of Arnold's rebellious feelings about his father's death in the prime of life when we read

> ... on the strenuous just man, Heaven bestows,
> Crown of his struggling life, an unjust close!)[2]

By 1849, when 'Resignation' was published at the end of his first volume of poems as a kind of testament, Arnold had certainly come to value detachment as a means of 'conquering fate', but here the technique of preaching to another what you still find difficult to accept yourself, or of reprobating in another the weaknesses identified in yourself—a technique familiar to us from Arnold's scolding of Clough in letters—is employed on Fausta

[1] Fragment clxxv. Long's translation (1877.)

[2] Dr. Arnold told his children stories from Herodotus at Fox How and set Mycerinus as the theme of the Rugby prize-poem in 1831. Matthew's poem is based on the account of Mycerinus in the second book of Herodotus.

(Jane Arnold), who is described as 'Time's chafing prisoner'. How remote Arnold's 'resignation' was from Stoic apathy, which involved a serene acceptance of the universal order, is underlined when he speaks with profound melancholy of

The something that infects the world.

What is evident in reading Arnold's first volume of poems, *The Strayed Reveller* (1849), is that his poetic development is less determined by aesthetic considerations than by the tension set up between these and his wish 'to get breast to breast with reality'. Even such narratives as 'Mycerinus' or 'The Sick King in Bokhara' and such tableaux as 'The Strayed Reveller' or 'The New Sirens' are patently something more than narratives or pictures, or, to put it another way, they have been adopted as subjects because they allow Arnold to experiment with different attitudes to life and estimate their adequacy.

'Empedocles on Etna' is seen in a true perspective as Arnold's most comprehensive attempt to '*solve* the Universe' by bringing into unity the fragments of his thought, but paradoxically it is the failure of this intention that is responsible finally for the artistic success of the poem. As a poet Arnold knew very well that a willed unity was only a shot-gun marriage to save appearances and insisted on rendering with integrity the 'alternating dispositions', the duality, the 'dialogue of the mind with itself',[1] of a divided nature.

II

In *A History of Western Philosophy* (1946) Bertrand Russell summarily dismissed 'Empedocles on Etna', which Arnold worked at for more than three years and made the title-poem of his second collection in 1852, as one of the poet's worst pieces. Since this judgement is at variance with that of most informed readers, whether they are admirers of Arnold's poetry or not, here, surely, the historian of philosophy has forgotten in his professional irritation that 'the truest poetry is the most feigning'. Arnold's Empedocles is obviously not the historical Empedocles: as J. C.

[1] 1853 Preface.

Shairp recognized in a letter to Clough when the poem had barely been begun, Arnold was using 'the name and outward circumstances' of the philosopher 'for the drapery of his own thoughts'.[1] If Arnold's Empedocles was meant to satisfy historians, he would not in Act II be such a blatant case-history of Romantic discouragement and dejection. Or again, if he was intended to be a faithful likeness of the author of the fragments of *On Nature* and the *Purifications*, the long philosophical discourse to Pausanias in Act I Scene ii would have to be characterized as a sustained anachronism. This rather glum 'sermon on the mount' (half-way up Etna) has one clear echo of the fragments of the real Empedocles, but, apart from some Epicurean elements derived from the *De Rerum Natura* of Lucretius and their distorted reflection in Senancour's *Obermann*, its basis is Stoic with a number of direct borrowings from Epictetus. To put the sentiments of Lucretius, who lived in the first half of the first century B.C., or of Epictetus, who was not born until a century after Lucretius died, into the mouth of a Sicilian philosopher of the fifth century B.C., who was the strict contemporary of Pericles, is as much an anachronism as to have a clock striking the hours in Shakespeare's *Julius Caesar*. Perhaps it is the kind of anachronism more likely to worry a philosopher than the ordinary student of literature.

Arnold would have pleaded poetic precedent for the historical liberties that he had taken with his subject, but he also believed that these liberties were less extreme than they appear to us. In a letter written in November 1867 he explains to a correspondent that before 'Empedocles on Etna' was written he 'had been much studying the remains of the early Greek religious philosophers' and had discovered in himself 'a sympathy with the figure Empedocles presents to the imagination'. He goes on to say that in portraying Empedocles he 'desired to gather up and draw out as a whole the hints which his remains offered'.[2] I think Arnold is being straightforward here, but I do not think he realized how ready he had been some fifteen years earlier to bring together

[1] *Correspondence of A. H. Clough*, ed. F. L. Mulhauser (1957), i, p. 280.

[2] *The Poetry of Matthew Arnold: a Commentary* by C. B. Tinker and H. F. Lowry (1940), pp. 287–8. Cited below as *Commentary*.

disparate ideas in his efforts to 'unite matter', or how slight the hints he had acted on might seem to anyone with a different mental history.

J. C. Shairp's letter of 30 June 1849 is the first reference to the composition of 'Empedocles on Etna'. The earliest mention of Empedocles as a poetic subject occurs on a list of poems to be written in 1849. The list, which probably belongs to late 1848, begins 'Chew Lucretius' and continues 'Compose 1. Empedocles —refusal of limitation by the religious sentiment'.[1] Shortly after *The Strayed Reveller* was published in February 1849 Arnold wrote to his mother, 'I had thoughts of publishing another volume of short poems next spring [1850], and a tragedy I have long had in mind the spring after [1851] . . . which however will not be a very quick affair'.[2] We may conclude that in February 'Empedocles' was to be a non-dramatic poem no longer than (say) 'Mycerinus', but that between then and the time of Shairp's letter in June the subject had so taken hold of Arnold's imagination that it had replaced 'Lucretius' as a main vehicle for his ideas and had become a 'dramatic poem'. The reading-lists in Arnold's early diaries show him studying the *De Rerum Natura* in 1845 and 1846,[3] and probably this is when he conceived the plan of writing a tragedy about Lucretius. Almost all that survives of this project belongs to Arnold's renewed work on the tragedy in 1855 or later, but the suggestion that the Roman play was to have 'a meditative, philosophical centre',[4] and that one reason for Arnold's failure ever to complete it was the incorporation of this philosophical material in 'Empedocles on Etna', is both plausible in itself and supported by the fact that drafts of two stanzas from Empedocles' discourse to Pausanias in Act I Scene ii were originally planned to belong to 'Lucretius'. We do not know why Arnold preferred Empedocles

[1] Yale MS.

[2] Mrs. Humphry Ward, *A Writer's Recollections* (1918), p. 43.

[3] See my article 'Matthew Arnold's Reading-Lists in Three Early Diaries', *Victorian Studies*, ii (1959), pp. 254–66. Cited below as 'Early Reading-Lists'. Dwight Culler has recently pointed out in *Imaginative Reason* (1966), p. 218, that Arnold borrowed volumes of Havercamp's edition of Lucretius from Oriel College library in October 1846 and July 1847.

[4] *Commentary*, p. 294.

to Lucretius in 1849, but we are safe in assuming that his interest in Empedocles was stimulated by the praise of the Sicilian philosopher in *De Rerum Natura*. Lucretius says of Empedocles that there is nothing in Sicily 'more illustrious than this man, nor more sacred and wonderful and dear' and that he announces his discoveries in such a manner that he seems 'hardly mortal'.[1] Writing to Clough in March 1848, Arnold distinguishes in Carlylean-Emersonian fashion between the 'philosophe' who trusts 'the logical absolute reason' and the 'philosopher' with insight who drives his feet 'into the solid ground of our individuality as spiritual, poetic, profound *persons*'.[2] As a poet in search of a philosophy he turned first and for preference to the insights of the poet-philosophers, who included for him the authors of the *Book of Job* and the Hindu *Bhagavad Gita* as well as Lucretius and Empedocles. In weighing these two it must have struck him that the Empedocles whom he described in the 1853 Preface as 'one of the last of the Greek religious philosophers, one of the family of Orpheus and Musaeus' was closer to his 1848 definition of the 'philosopher' than the Epicurean Lucretius whose enthusiasm for science and contempt for religion give him a look of the Voltairean 'philosophe'. We know now that Arnold's interest in the *Bhagavad Gita* had been aroused by October 1845 and that it increased when he read the poem and what had been written about it. He shows his familiarity with the poem's ideas when early in 1848 he tries to convert Clough to his own enthusiasm.[3] Victor Cousin seems to have directed him to Wilhelm von Humboldt's analysis of the *Bhagavad Gita* in the *Transactions of the Royal Academy of the Sciences*, Berlin (1826).[4] This analysis contains, as does H. H. Milman's review of it and other works on Hindu poetry in the *Quarterly Review* of April 1831, which Arnold certainly read, the assertion of a likeness between the *Bhagavad Gita*, the *De Rerum Natura* and the fragments of Empedocles. Milman, who was Professor of Poetry at Oxford when he wrote

[1] *De Rerum Natura*, i, 726–33.
[2] Lowry, p. 73.
[3] Lowry, pp. 69 and 71.
[4] 'Early Reading-Lists', *Victorian Studies*, ii (1959), p. 261

this review, says that the Hindu 'divine song' in its place in the *Mahabharata* 'reads like a noble fragment of Empedocles or Lucretius introduced into the midst of an Homeric epic', and that in its freedom from 'redundance of metaphor' it is 'Grecian rather than Italian' in taste.[1] Associations between Lucretius, Empedocles and the *Bhagavad Gita* had been formed in Arnold's mind before he began to study the Greek philosopher.

Arnold studied Empedocles in Simon Karsten's edition (Amsterdam, 1838),[2] which provides an introduction ('De Empedoclis Vita et Studiis'), a Latin translation of the fragments printed opposite the Greek text, detailed notes, and a long essay on the philosopher's ideas. Students of Arnold know of this edition, but they have not used it. Examination of it shows that the 'hints' Arnold claimed to have found in the philosopher's remains come in many instances from Karsten's introduction and final essay. For example, the characterization of Empedocles in the 1853 Preface as 'one of the last of the Greek religious philosophers' derives directly from Karsten's description of Empedocles as 'almost the last of those poet-prophets . . . of the line of Orpheus . . . who instruct and govern the ignorant and simple by sacred ordinances and songs'.[3] Again, there is nothing in the fragments or in the account of Empedocles by Diogenes Laertius to suggest the melancholy disposition and vast discouragement which Arnold fastens on his hero—indeed it is accepted that Arnold has simply tranferred to the philosopher 'the feeling of depression, the feeling of *ennui*' which he found 'stamped on the poem of Lucretius'.[4] Yet even for this transfer he found 'hints' in the facts of Empedocles' life—in his exile, in his being one of the *last* of the old Greek religious philosophers (which immediately suggested to Arnold a man 'wandering between two worlds'); in Karsten's description of the philosopher's lofty solemnity and arrogance

---

[1] *Quarterly Review*, xlv (April 1831), pp. 3–4, 7.

[2] *Philosophorum Graecorum Veterum . . . Operum Reliquiae*, ii (1838). Cited below as 'Karsten'.

[3] Karsten, p. 33. My own translation.

[4] 'On the Modern Element in Literature' (1857), *Prose Works*, i (1960), p. 32.

(which made Arnold speak of Empedocles' 'proud sad face'); and in Aristotle's judgement reported by Karsten that the soul of Empedocles was μελαγχολικός. These are some of the 'hints' which permitted Arnold to connect the historical Empedocles with Lucretius and present his own Empedocles as one in whose work 'we hear already the doubts, we witness the discouragement, of Hamlet and Faust'.[1]

The melancholy of Arnold's Empedocles is the Romantic melancholy of Byron's *Manfred*, of George Sand's *Lélia*, of Foscolo's *Ultime Lettere di Jacopo Ortis*, and, above all, of Senancour's *Obermann*. When Arnold said in 1857 that 'the feeling of depression, the feeling of *ennui*' was 'stamped on how many of the representative works of modern times'[2] it was of these and similar books that he was thinking. That Empedocles is identified with Senancour through Lucretius is plain when we notice in 'Empedocles on Etna' that Callicles corrects Pausanias, who supposes simple-mindedly that Empedocles' trouble is that the times are out of joint, with the words:

> 'Tis not the times, 'tis not the sophists vex him;
> There is some root of suffering in himself,
> · Some secret and unfollow'd vein of woe,
> Which makes the time look black and sa dto him . . .
>   [I. i. 150–53]

and then discover that Arnold echoes these words in his 1869 essay on *Obermann*:

> But a root of failure, powerlessness, and ennui, there certainly was in the constitution of Senancour's own nature; so that, unfavourable as may have been his time, we should err in attributing to any outward circumstances the whole of the discouragement by which he is pervaded.[3]

From the link Arnold established in his mind between the

[1] 1853 Preface.
[2] 'On the Modern Element in Literature', Prose Works, i (1960), p. 32.
[3] *Essays, Letters, and Reviews by Matthew Arnold*, ed. F. Neiman (1960), p. 161.

fragments of Empedocles and the *Bhagavad Gita* we can understand Clough's gibe in his notice of 'Empedocles on Etna' in the *North American Review* in 1853 at 'the dismal cycle' of Arnold's 're-habilitated Hindoo-Greek theosophy'.[1] The pantheist notion of 'A God identical with the world and with the sum of force therein contained: not exterior to it',[2] which is expressed in Arnold's poem in the lines

> All things the world which fill
> Of but one stuff are spun,
> That we who rail are still,
> With what we rail at, one . . . , [I. ii. 287–90]

derives multiply from a fragment of Empedocles ('. . . . but [God] is only sacred and ineffable mind, penetrating the whole world with rapid thought'),[3] from Arjuna's vision in the *Bhagavad Gita* of the universe 'standing in a vast unity in the body of the God of gods', from the Stoic doctrine of the World-Soul and Spinoza's 'Deus, sive Natura', and from Wordsworth's and Goethe's poems, although we should also note that Arnold's actual words seem to echo Emerson's 'Nature', which was included in *Essays* (1844):

> . . . she [Nature] has but one stuff to serve all her dream-like variety. Compound it how she will . . . it is still but one stuff.[4]

Obermann in his pilgrimage to the Dent du Midi reminds Sainte-Beuve of the Lucretian sage raised above the tumult of life: 'S'il s'élançait, s'il disparaissait alors, ce serait presque en Dieu, comme Empédocle à l'Etna'.[5] He wanders like Byron's Manfred

---

[1] *Poems and Prose Remains of A. H. Clough* (1869), i, p. 378.

[2] Yale MS.

[3] Karsten, p. 138. Fragment 360.

[4] *Complete Works of R. W. Emerson* (Bohn's Standard Library edn., 1881), i, p. 229.

[5] *Les Grands Écrivains Français par Sainte-Beuve*, ed. M. Allem. XIXᵉ Siècle: *Les Romanciers* (1927), i, p.57. Sainte-Beuve's essay was first published in 1832 and was read by Arnold in the first volume of *Portraits Contemporains* (1845).

in the Alps, suffering like George Sand's Lélia from 'l'excès de douleur produit par l'abus de la pensée'. His mind is 'over-tasked' —to use the word Adrnol applied to both Lucretius and Empedocles. Manfred and Obermann were remembered by Arnold when 'in a curious and not altogether comfortable state' he wandered about Thun in 1849 and longed to carry his 'aching head to the mountains'.[1] He felt himself 'over-tasked'. 'Yes,' he writes to Clough in February 1853, '*congestion of the brain* is what we suffer from—I always feel it and say it—and cry for air like my own Empedocles.'[2] The network of associated ideas and images drawn from Arnold's reading and personal experience that lies behind 'Empedocles on Etna' is far more complicated than I have attempted to show, but even so simplified a diagram of it would justify us in speaking of the poem as a culmination of Arnold's earlier poetic efforts to 'unite matter' and 'get breast to breast with reality'.

'Empedocles on Etna' is not what the Arnold who sought an 'intellectual deliverance' wanted to say, but what the truth-telling poet was unable not to say. His philosopher is wretched and cannot live by the philosophy of resignation that he preaches. Arnold states in his plans for the poem in the Yale MS. that the vision of 'the stern simplicity' of the real nature of things is 'capable of affording rapture and the purest peace', but he did not feel that rapture or experience that peace. He tries hard to make Empedocles a special case by the very variety of the reasons that he adduces to explain his hero's loss of 'spring and elasticity of mind', but the truth is that despondency is more real to him than the sentiment that 'Life still/Leaves human effort scope'. The ascent of the volcano from the shady, moist 'forest region' at its foot to the 'charr'd, blacken'd, melancholy waste' of the cone becomes a secular Way of the Cross that ends in self-crucifixion. The ascent re-enacts the journey of the Romantic poet from innocence (Callicles) to experience (Empedocles)—

---

[1] Lowry, p. 110. Byron's *Manfred*, as I have shown elsewhere, determined the choice of dramatic form for 'Empedocles on Etna' and the evolution of the action—see *Notes and Queries*, *n.s.*, ix (1962), pp. 300–3.

[2] Lowry, p. 130.

We Poets in our youth begin in gladness;
But thereof come in the end despondency and madness...[1]

and also, more broadly, symbolizes what may happen to a man
when he leaves behind as illusions the religious beliefs which have
hitherto given his life significance (by being accepted unquestion-
ingly) and moves into what W. B. Yeats calls 'the desolation of
reality'. Empedocles 'sees things as they are', but the vision is too
much for him. The movement from innocence to experience,
from the comfort of traditional beliefs to the painful vision of
reality, is a movement in time that the poem renders spatially. At
one pitch of generalization 'Empedocles on Etna' is a poem about
the cruelty of time, and there is more irony than resignation in
Arnold's adoption of a saying attributed to Thales in Diogenes
Laertius' *Lives of the Philosophers*, 'Time is the wisest of things, for
it finds out everything' as a motto for his 1852 volume. Nothing
in Arnold's letters strikes the reader with more force than his
repeated complaints about the loss of youth, which are the shadow
of a pre-lapsarian happiness:

> And yet what days were those, Parmenides!
> When we were young ...

> Then we could still enjoy, then neither thought
> Nor outward things were closed and dead to us;
> But we received the shock of mighty thoughts
> On simple minds with a pure natural joy ...
>   [II [i] 235-6, 240-3]

There is a passage in what Arnold calls Sainte-Beuve's 'very good
article'[2] on Leopardi in the fourth volume of *Portraits Contemporains* which must have seemed to Arnold a wording of his most
intimate doubts and fears. Sainte-Beuve writes:

> Il me semble que, lorsqu'on se met en rapport par la croyance,
> par la prière ... avec la grande âme du monde, on trouve appui

---

[1] Wordworth's 'Resolution and Independence'.

[2] In his notice of Sainte-Beuve for the *Encyclopaedia Britannica* in 1886.

accord, apaisement. Que si la créature humaine s'en détache au contraire et ne trouve pas de raison suffisante pour croire et pour espérer, comme à la rigeur elle en a peut-être le droit, car les preuves de raisonnement laissent á désirer, elle en est à l'instant punie par je ne sais quoi d'aride et de désolé.[1]

Arnold's own version of these reflections appears in a note in the Yale MS. (undated, but almost certainly written between 1849 and 1852):

> I cannot conceal from myself that the objection which really wounds and perplexes me from the religious side is that the service of reason is freezing to feeling, chilling to the religious mood.
> And feeling and the religious mood are eternally the deepest being of man, the ground of all joy and greatness for him.

'Empedocles on Etna' was rejected as a failure because it left Arnold with a hopeless antinomy: on the one hand, 'the pale cold star of Truth' to be followed; on the other hand, the necessity of joy. But joy is impossible if 'the service of reason' freezes 'feeling and the religious mood'; and the price of joy is beyond the means of the sensitive and honest man if payment has to be made in the currency of illusion. However hard he tried, Arnold could not embrace 'truth' and 'joy' in a single thought, but was drawn back again and again to the nagging contradiction between them:

> And yet men have such need of joy!
> But joy whose grounds are true . . .[2]

He turned away from the contradiction that had nerved his most complex work by discarding 'Empedocles on Etna' in 1853 and defending his rejection of it in a preface which, as a modern critic has said, was 'written by Arnold's spectre'.[3] It was like the crisis of a long and punishing illness from which the patient recovers to

[1] The essay is dated 1844. Quoted here from the 1884 edn. of *Portraits Contemporains*, iv, p. 411.

[2] 'Obermann Once More', ll. 237-8.

[3] Frank Kermode, *The Romantic Image* (1957), p. 12.

lead a diminished life. The new poems that Arnold wrote after 1852 took less out of him. Gradually there were fewer poems and in the end no poems at all. The nostalgic prefatory quatrain to *New Poems* (1867) shows that Arnold recognized fully what was happening:

> Though the Muse be gone away,
> Though she move not earth today,
> Souls, erewhile who caught her word,
> Ah! still harp on what they heard.

III

After his marriage in June 1851 (when he was still engaged in writing 'Empedocles on Etna') and the start of his new duties as a school inspector, Arnold had less time to devote to poetry than in his bachelor days, but the real impediments to poetic composition were not external. The increasing difficulty Arnold found in writing poetry after 'Empedocles on Etna' was not a matter of busy tours of inspection, bad hotels and snatched meals (he produced a fair quota of poetic work when conditions were worst in the early years of his appointment), but was due ultimately to his decision to hold back something of himself in the act of creation (which is the true meaning to be attached to the rejection of subjectivity in the 1853 Preface), and this decision is connected with his need to settle down, come to terms with ordinary life, and 'mature'. It seems, he writes bleakly to his sister Jane a few months before his marriage (25 January 1851), '. . . as if we could only acquire any solidity of shape and power of acting by narrowing and narrowing our sphere', but how reluctantly he faced this prospect is evident when he adds that he is 'almost tempted to quarrel with the law of nature' which compels us to leave 'the aimless and unsettled, but also open and liberal of our youth' and 'take refuge in our morality and character'.[1] It was to the same sister in September 1858 that he acknowledged that his tragedy *Merope* (1858) belonged to a less ambitious kind

[1] *Letters of Matthew Arnold*, ed. G. W. E. Russell (1895), i, p. 14. Cited below as *Letters*.

of poetry than 'Empedocles on Etna' and stood in need of apology.

> People do not understand what a temptation there is, if you cannot bear anything not *very good*,.to transfer your operations to a region where form is everything. Perfection of a certain kind may there be attained, or at least approached, without knocking yourself to pieces, but to attain or approach perfection in the region of thought and feeling, and to unite this with perfection of form, demands not merely an effort and a labour, but an actual tearing of oneself to pieces, which one does not readily consent to (although one is sometimes forced to it) unless one can devote one's whole life to poetry.[1]

I find this letter moving, especially Arnold's confession that he is still sometimes forced in spite of himself 'to submit . . . to the exhaustion of the best poetical production'. In 'an existence so hampered as mine is'—he was now a man with a family to support who for financial reasons had taken on the extra task of acting as Marshal when his father-in-law Judge Wightman was on circuit— he pleads that he can no longer bear the labour-pains of poetic creation, which are 'an actual tearing of oneself to pieces'. Not only is his existence hampered, but the times are against him (as they were against Empedocles). He claims that it is 'only in the best poetical epochs (such as the Elizabethan) that you can descend into yourself and produce the best of your thought and feeling naturally, and without an overwhelming and in some degree morbid effort'.[2]

It is important to understand what Arnold is saying. He was not Gautier, a poet whom he did not care for, or Mallarmé, whom he would not have understood. When he speaks of transferring his operations to 'a region where form is everything' he is not slighting the importance of his dramatic subject in *Merope*—a subject which he had chosen with great care, if rather absurdly, from a number listed in Hyginus, 'a Latin mythographer of uncertain

---

[1] *Letters*, i, pp. 62–3 (where the letter is misdated '6 August' instead of '6 September').

[2] All the quotations in this paragraph are from the same letter of 6 September 1858.

date',[1] because it seemed to him to contain an 'excellent action', that is to say, one with a powerful appeal 'to the great primary human affections: to those elementary feelings which subsist permanently in the race, and which are independent of time'.[2] A 'region where form is everything' must be translated as 'a region where the artist's struggle is exclusively with form and expression because the subject does not involve the perplexities of his own development'. This is, of course, the 1853 Preface's denial that a poem should be 'a true allegory of the state of one's own mind'.[3] The pseudo-classicism of the preface must therefore be seen as a direct evasion of the strains and anxieties of genuine poetic creation.

Merope, which is by common consent a poetic failure, lies at the far end of the line on which 'Sohrab and Rustum', which took the place of 'Empedocles on Etna' in Arnold's 1853 volume, and 'Balder Dead' (1855) are important intermediate stations. Both these poems have some poetic value because Arnold was able to connect their 'excellent actions' with his own experience, because, in other words, the poems retain in spite of Arnold's infatuation with a chimerical pure objectivity a subjective element. (A purely objective poem is by definition a dead poem, since it has not engaged the poet and therefore cannot be expected to interest his readers.) Arnold's letter of 6 September 1858 admits implicitly that 'Empedocles on Etna' is a poem in which its author had struggled to 'approach perfection in the region of thought and feeling' and to 'unite this with perfection of form', and that this struggle had been 'not merely an effort and a labour, but an actual tearing of [himself] to pieces'. *Merope* was written to 'inaugurate my Professorship with dignity'[4]—Arnold had been elected Professor of Poetry at Oxford some eight months earlier on 5 May

---

[1] Preface to *Merope*.

[2] 1833 Preface.

[3] Ibid. Arnold is quoting a phrase from David Masson's 'Theories of Poetry and a New Poet', *North British Review*, xix (August 1853), p. 338. The phrase caught Arnold on the raw because it was so apt a description of 'Empedocles on Etna'.

[4] *Letters*, i, p. 60.

1857. 'Empedocles on Etna' was written because there was no escape from it, because, as Arnold told Clough in December 1852, '. . . woe was upon me if I analysed not my situation'.[1] It is a remarkable if unintentional irony, then, that these two pieces—the one, though flawed, written at the height of his powers, the other the most frigid of all his compositions—should in Arnold's final classification of his poetry in 1885 occupy a special category by themselves as 'dramatic poems'.

[1] Lowry, p. 126.

VI

A. C. Bradley's 'Shakespearean Tragedy'[1]

G. K. HUNTER

A. C. BRADLEY'S *Shakespearean Tragedy* stands on the book-shelves like one of the more ponderous and irremovable monuments of the late Victorian establishment, overshadowing what has followed it, and none the less resented for that. The clerihew in which Shakespeare sits for a Civil Service Exam, '. . . In which Shakespeare did very badly/Because he hadn't studied Bradley'/ catches very well this image of the book as an Establishment synthesis,[2] making possible the absorption of Shakespeare into the higher educational system, long dominated by the Greats syllabus of Classics and Philosophy. Bradley himself, classicist and philosopher, was an obvious person to effect this sea-change in Shakespeare study.

As I suggest, most references to Bradley's book since the time of its publication have been either resentful of its influence or (alternatively) defensive about its virtues. I wish here to take up neither of these roles; but, accepting *Shakespearean Tragedy* as one of the classics of English criticism, to ask what kind of book it is, and how it came to possess the qualities that characterize it. This involves a look at its author.

Andrew Cecil Bradley was born in 1851 into the already extensive family of the Reverend Charles Bradley, an Evangelical clergyman of some fame as a sermon-writer. The Reverend Charles looks from this distance like a caricature of all that we

---

[1] Given originally as a lecture at the Royal Shakespeare Theatre Summer School, September 1964.

[2] Cf. *The Times Literary Supplement*, 23 May 1936: 'the critic recognises . . . that in so far as he agrees with Bradley he is mature; and where he disagrees he has still a long road to travel. But he makes no doubt that the road will lead him to Bradley again, and bring him under that sign to the thrill of critical certitude, and the bliss of critical peace'.

suppose Victorian clergymen to have been—forceful, long-lived, dogmatic, a domestic tyrant,[1] whose first wife 'succumbed before the advent of her fourteenth baby'[2] and whose second wife raised the total of his children to some twenty-two. The children were moreover destined to spread their competence over large areas of late Victorian intellectual life. George Granville Bradley, the fourth son of the first marriage, born some thirty years before Andrew Cecil, became Headmaster of Marlborough College in 1858, and Master of University College, Oxford, in 1870. He was to go on to become Dean of Westminster in succession to Arthur Stanley, whose life he wrote. His children were A. C. Bradley's contemporaries; several of them (for example, Arthur Granville Bradley and (Daisy) Margaret Louisa Woods) became literary figures in their own right. The atmosphere of the family may be gauged from the magazine *The Miscellany*, which was edited by two daughters of G. G. Bradley in the years 1867–1873.[3] This had a list of subscribers and of contributors that would be the delight of any modern professional and metropolitan effort —including two that Edith Bradley was later to call 'our father's brilliant young step-brothers, the younger of whom was not only near my own age, but a warm and close friend'.[4] The two step-brothers were Francis Herbert Bradley, the Idealist Philosopher and valetudinarian Fellow of Merton, born in 1846, and Andrew Cecil Bradley, whose contributions to *The Miscellany* are interesting supplements to the corpus of his literary criticism. F. H. Bradley was at Oxford at the same time as Andrew Bradley, moved in the same crucial circles; they remained close enough for the younger brother to take responsibility for the second edition of *Ethical Studies* in 1927.

This description of the family circle should not end without the mention of one other member, Sir George Grove, civil engineer, musicologist, editor, founder and first Principal of the Royal College of Music. Grove had grown up in Clapham, that hotbed

[1] See G. R. G. Mure, 'F. H. Bradley', *Encounter*, XVI (1961), p. 28.
[2] See Bodleian MS. Don. d 129, fol 154.
[3] Now in the Bodleian Library as Bodl. MS Don. e 35, d 196.
[4] Edith Nicholl Ellison, *A Child's Recollection of Tennyson* (1907).

of Evangelical piety, where the Reverend Charles Bradley had had a chapel (St. James's, Clapham) built for him by his admiring flock; Grove married Harriet Bradley, and towards the end of the century he seems to have been close friend of Andrew Bradley; he published several signed articles by his brother-in-law in *Macmillan's Magazine* while he was its editor; Germanic and musical interests were among the bonds that tied the two men together.

By the time A. C. Bradley was born, the Reverend Charles had moved from Clapham to Cheltenham, and it was at Cheltenham College (for boys) that Andrew was educated. What seems crucial in the formation of his intellectual position was, however, what followed the schooling.

Between school and Oxford (to which he went in 1869) Bradley had some free time; and it is in this period that Mackail[1] locates a spiritual crisis—'a strong, even violent reaction from the atmosphere of rigid evangelicalism in which he had grown up'. Much of his intellectual position in later years is to be explained by the rejection of this form of faith, with its emphasis on the literal truth of scripture, the need for a personal sense of sin and a personal path to salvation, its insistence on the miraculous, supernatural and irrational quality of conventional religious life. The reaction against a dominant Evangelical father is a standard enough Victorian pattern which few intellectuals of the time seem to have avoided. The particular form the story took in the life of A. C. Bradley—a form that leads directly, I believe, to *Shakespearean Tragedy*—is to be explained by the influences he met when he carried his spiritual crisis to Balliol in 1869.

Fifty years later Bradley was to tell a friend that his soul had been saved by Thomas Hill Green.[2] Green, himself the son of an Evangelical parson, had come to Balliol in 1855, and he was elected Fellow in 1860. He became the centre of an Oxford attachment to German Idealist philosophy, but was perhaps even more influential as a living testimony to the ethical power possible outside supernatural sanctions.

[1] 'Andrew Cecil Bradley', *Proceedings of the British Academy* XXI (1935).
[2] Ibid., p. 386.

Edward Caird says in the preface to Seth and Haldane's *Essays in Philosophical Criticism* (1883), a memorial volume by Green's former pupils:

> To Professor Green philosophy was not a study of the words of men that are gone but a life transmitted from them to him—a a life expressing itself with that power and authority which belongs to one who speaks from his own experience and never to 'the scribes' who speak from tradition.

Again, and even more extremely:

> There are not a few among the Oxford men of the last fifteen years to whom . . . his existence was one of the things that gave reality to the distinction between good and evil.

But perhaps the most eloquent description of Green's effect on men of Bradley's generation is to be found in Mrs. Humphrey Ward's *Robert Elsmere*, where Mr. Grey represents T. H. Green. The young Robert Elsmere attends a lay sermon by Grey and is immediately bowled over by the force of this new call to self sacrifice:

> How the 'pitiful earthy self' with its passions and its cravings sank into nothingness beside the 'great ideas' and the 'great causes' for which, as Christians and as men he claimed their devotion.

Shortly afterwards Elsmere describes Grey/Green's intellectual position more explicitly:

> The whole basis of Grey's thought was ardently idealist and Hegelian. He had broken with the popular Christianity, but for him, God, consciousness, duty, were the only realities. None of the various forms of materialist thought escaped his challenge; no genuine utterance of the spiritual life of man but was sure of his sympathy.

To ardent souls brought up in the hectic atmosphere of Evangelical charity, but unwilling to accept supernatural sanctions, Green managed to suggest a new set of ethical imperatives, a new sense of guilt, a new call to the higher life. 'He gave us back the language of self-sacrifice,' said one of his pupils, quoted by Mr. Melvin Richter. The world was still full of evils that the good man had to fight; but the path of combat Green indicated did not lead to Rome; but to Stepney, to Toynbee Hall, to female emancipation and the University Extension Lectures Movement.

Bradley's debt to Green is quite explicit—he was one of the small inner circle of disciples—and he remained under the spell of Green's 'metaphysics of morality' for the rest of his life. The set of Gifford lectures he delivered in Glasgow in 1907—published in 1940 by his sister, Marian de Glehn, under the title *Ideals of Religion*—is still entirely Greenian in its devotion to the concept of God as the highest realization of the inner self. And in the same lectures we may notice the Greenian point that the universal good can often be achieved only by the surrender or sacrifice of individual happiness or prosperity—but then the sacrifice of individual goods is in the highest sense 'good'. The relation of this to the famous 'substance of tragedy' chapter in *Shakespearean Tragedy* is sufficiently obvious not to require further comment.

In 1915 Bradley gave a lecture in Bedford College, London, on 'International Morality: the United States of Europe'. The intellectual framework of his remarks here is still the same—Aristotle, F. H. Bradley, Green, Bosanquet, Green again. It is obvious that Bradley did not discover new allegiances in the second half of his life, but remained essentially a part of the Oxford circle (Bosanquet, F. H. Bradley, Nettleship, Arnold Toynbee, J. H. Muirhead, Edward Caird, Charles Gore, *et al.*) he knew in the eighteen seventies. It is not really surprising that Bradley's mind remained dyed in Green's colouring. Not only was he devoted to him as a pupil and a colleague, but he was involved in publishing Green's *Prolegomena* after the latter's death in 1882. The editorial process is likely to render ideas indelible; but martyrdom leaves an even deeper impress; and Bradley seems to have suffered some kind of martyrdom in Oxford because of his devotion to Green. Benjamin Jowett, from 1870 onward the Master of Balliol, was opposed to Green's tendency to systematize and to gather disciples who believed in his system. Jowett thought of philosophy as a school of scepticism; and believed that the tutor should leave the pupil's mind free to form individual opinions. Green's younger disciples —Nettleship and Bradley—seem never to have enjoyed the Master's confidence.[1] Bradley's teaching career in Balliol must have been frustrating. In 1875 he was offered a History lectureship if he spent two semesters in a German University.[2] Accordingly he went in 1875 to Berlin. But from another letter of slightly later date it appears that he is still suspect as a possible *proselytizer*. He says 'I must try to convince him [Jowett] that I can attend to grammar and I do not want to proselytize'. He *did* lecture on Aristotle's *Ethics*—some shorthand notes of his lectures survive—but the Master's opposition does not seem to have dissolved.

A letter from Green dated 23 June 1881 implies that about 1876 Bradley had been offered a lectureship at New College and that Green had persuaded him to stay in Balliol. Green goes on:

> I did not then forecast the financial future of the College or the persistency of the Master's opposition—not as it is needless to say to you personally—but to that kind of teaching being given in the College in which you could be most useful.[3]

He mentions the possibility of Bradley applying for a Chair of literature in the new University College in Liverpool ('Enquire carefully about the climate'). Bradley pursued the Liverpool possibility ('So far as I was able to learn there is nothing very deterrent about the climate of Liverpool'), and states clearly enough his reasons for moving:

[1] Letter from J. A. Symonds to Mrs. Green, cited in Melvin Richter, *The Politics of Conscience* (1964), p. 392, n. 22.

[2] MS. letter from Bradley to Green (May or June 1875) in Balliol College Library.

[3] MS. letter from Green to Bradley (dated 23 June 1881) in Balliol College Library.

Some amount of collision with the Master will I foresee be inevitable if I stay. I do not think I can teach more with a view to the examination than I have.[1]

Bradley's move from philosophy at Oxford to literature at Liverpool was to prove a fortunate one for English scholarship, but it came about fortuitously enough. Two Chairs were available: one of Philosophy and Political Economy, another of Modern Literature and History. Bradley was puzzled to know which fitted him better (or worse). He had been, throughout his time at Balliol, a philosopher above all. In his application to Liverpool he said that 'during the last nine years I have worked most at philosophy, especially in its application to morals, politics and literature'.[2] His references (all twenty-eight of them!) are predominantly concerned with his philosophical abilities, which are described in terms not very different from those earlier applied to Green. For example, he is called 'a man . . . to whom philosophy is not a set of abstractions but a life'.[3] J. H. Muirhead describes the surprise of Oxford men of the time that Bradley should have obtained the Literature Chair and not the Philosophy one, while his Balliol colleague, John MacCunn, became Professor of Philosophy.[4]

Bradley had, in fact, displayed his literary leanings before this time. I have already mentioned his essays in *The Miscellany*. S. H. Butcher, in a reference written for him when he applied for the Merton Chair of English in 1885, says that he had known Bradley 'from the time when as a boy at school he already possessed a knowledge of English literature that was quite unusual at such an age'. Butcher goes on to tell us that 'in 1879 he was invited by the Committee of the Association for Promoting the Higher Education of women in Oxford to lecture for them on English Litera-

---

[1] MS. letter from Bradley to Green (27 September 1881) in Balliol College Library.

[2] Testimonials in favour of A. C. Bradley (*Applications for the English Chair at Liverpool*, 1881) in the Bodleian Library.

[3] Letter of recommendation from R. G. Tatton, printed with the above.

[4] J. H. Muirhead, *Reflections of a Journeyman in Philosophy* (1942), pp. 41, 48f.

H

ture'.[1] He had already contributed essays on Marlowe and on Beaumont and Fletcher to T. H. Ward's *Selections from the English Poets* (1880) and on Browning and on Mythological Poetry to *Macmillan's Magazine*. He tells us himself that in 1877 he was invited to meet Swinburne: 'Jowett was then Master, and I a young don whom he knew to be interested in poetry.'[2]

So began the career of lectures—we hear of Liverpool lectures on 'Socrates', 'Mazzini', 'The Study of Poetry', 'Shakespeare', 'Cowper', 'Wordsworth and Coleridge', Tennyson's *In Memoriam*[3]—which carried him from Liverpool to Glasgow in 1889 and, after he had resigned the Glasgow Chair in 1900, through his stint as Professor of Poetry at Oxford, 1901–6. These finally emerged in publication as *Shakespearean Tragedy* and *Oxford Lectures on Poetry*. A last gleaning of his lectures appeared in *A Miscellany*—a volume of less sustained excellence than the other two. Subsequently, his retirement 'to devote himself to leisured critical work'[4] was not broken; it seems probable that the collapse of his Germanophile intellectual world in the 1914–18 war was answered by some decline in his intellectual powers.[5] He lived until 1935, but wrote no more (so far as we know), shielded from scrutiny by his sister, Marian de Glehn.

I have dwelt at length on Bradley's philosophical allegiances, for these are central, I believe, to an explanation of his literary criticism, and in particular to an explanation of the most sustained critical exercise of his life—*Shakespearean Tragedy*. Throughout his life he was proud to think of himself as a philosopher-critic. At the end of his Oxford lectures he defended his 'propensity to philosophize' with the credo that Oxford's 'best intellectual gift was the conviction that what imagination loved as poetry reason

---

[1] Testimonials in favour of A. C. Bradley (*Applications for the Merton Chair of English in 1885*) in the Bodleian Library.

[2] E. Gosse, *Swinburne* (1917), pp. 296f.

[3] Letters from Joshua Sing and H. C. Beeching, included in n. 2, p. 107 above.

[4] M. R. Ridley in *DNB, 1931–1940*.

[5] 'the strain of the war on him was great and he never quite recovered from it' (Mackail, in *Proceedings of the British Academy, XXI* (1935), p. 391).

might love as philosophy'. Dealing with Shakespeare, Bradley seems to start from his imaginative response to the tragic power of his poetry; and the effort of *Shakespearean Tragedy* is then, in terms of this equation, to transmute this response into a rational and systematized account of what is there, without loss and without falsification.

But Shakespearean tragedy is no accidental resting-place for Bradley's critical powers. The world of these tragedies is remarkably apposite to the systems of thought to which he was most attached and to the mode in which his mind worked most fruitfully. M. R. Ridley had noticed that even among the diverse essays of the *Oxford Lectures* Shakespeare occupies a prominent place, and that the Shakespearean subjects seem to call out a fuller measure of critical power than do the others. We may make the same point in another way: certain subjects do not seem to have elicited Bradley's response. Of these the most notable, and I believe the most significant, is Milton. It is apparent from a sentence at the end of 'Shelley's view of poetry' that Bradley was offended by the explicit dogmatisms of *Paradise Lost*:

> Milton was far from justifying the ways of God to men by the argumentation he put into divine and angelic lips; his truer moral insight is in the creations of his genius; for instance, in the character of Satan or the picture of the glorious humanity of Adam and Eve.

With this slender hold on the range of *Paradise Lost* we may feel that Bradley was well justified in his Miltonic abstinence. But we should further notice that Shakespeare possesses perfectly what Milton is censured for lacking, a world fraught with spiritual meaning, but never explicit, a world of 'modern' realities—and here obviously superior to Greek tragedies, as on the other 'spiritual' side it is superior to the world of the novelists.

A remarkable essay on 'Old Mythology in Modern Poetry', published by Bradley in *Macmillan's Magazine*, vol. 44 (1881), when his brother-in-law George Grove was editor, indicates some of the reasons why Shakespearean Tragedy was so perfectly appropriate to his philosophic interests. The essay is concerned with the relation between belief and understanding, between the religious and the aesthetic senses, and pursues the tendency of religious beliefs to turn into poetic mythologies. The final section of the essay deplores the tendency of modern poets to draw on remote mythologies:

> Art had two great enemies, the dominion of theology and the prejudices of aristocracy: She has freed herself from both, and should look at life with open eyes. Why, most of all, not content with

> Jove, Apollo, Mars and such raskaille,

> should we interpose the shapes of eastern and northern mythology between ourselves and reality, and even attempt to preserve those portions of our own religious ideas, the disappearance of which we ought to welcome? (p. 47)

If Bradley is asking here (as I suppose) that the mythological or poetic-religious perceptions of modern poets should refer to real life, it is interesting that he goes on to invoke Shakespeare as an exponent of this activity: '. . . they can appeal for confirmation of its dignity to the greatest name in all literature.' In the language of this article, Shakespeare's tragic world seems to have the powerful recommendation that it is both real and factual and, at the same time, to be employing its realities as a mode of mythology, as a way of telling us about the general truths of the universe. I assume that Bradley is drawing on the same nomenclature when in an obscure passage of *Shakespearean Tragedy* he tells us that fate in Shakespeare

> appears to be a mythological expression for the whole system or order, of which the individual characters form an inconsiderable and feeble part. (p. 30)

The tragedies as wholes have *meanings*, and the meanings far transcend the individual parts, the individual opinions of the characters; but this meaning is, like the meaning of a mythology, only to be inferred from the surface facts; it cannot be proved to exist, but its effects can be felt and responded to, and in terms of the ideal critic 'loved as philosophy'.

> 'What a piece of work is man,' we cry; 'so much more beautiful and so much more terrible than we knew! Why should he be so if this beauty and greatness only tortures itself and throws itself away?' We seem to have before us a type of the mystery of the whole world, the tragic fact which extends far beyond the limits of tragedy. Everywhere, from the crushed rocks beneath our feet to the soul of man, we see power, intelligence, life and glory, which astound us and seem to call for our worship. And everywhere we see them perishing, devouring one another and destroying themselves, often with dreadful pain, as though they came into being for no other end. Tragedy is the typical form of this mystery, because that greatness of soul which it exhibits oppressed, conflicting and destroyed, is the highest existence in our view. (p. 23)

The poetic power of the tragic world gives an especially cogent image of the human mystery that had faced Bradley from the time of coming up to Oxford. Moreover, it is an image of that world which rules out, by its nature, the orthodox religious answers that he had long ago abandoned as inappropriate. In the opening lecture he speaks of the basic question 'regarding the tragic world and the ultimate power in it' and then goes on to indicate some of the conditions involved in a satisfactory answer to this question:

> It will be agreed, however, first, that this question must not be answered in 'religious' language. For although this or that *dramatis persona* may speak of gods or of God, of evil spirits or of Satan, of heaven and of hell, and although the poet may show us ghosts from another world, these ideas do not materially influence his representation of life, nor are they used to throw light on the mystery of its tragedy. The Elizabethan drama was almost wholly secular; and while Shakespeare was writing he practically confined his view to the world of non-theological observation and thought, so that he represents it substantially in

one and the same way whether the period of the story is pre-Christian or Christian.[1] He looked at this 'secular' world most intently and seriously; and he painted it, we cannot but conclude, with entire fidelity, without the wish to enforce an opinion of his own, and, in essentials, without regard to anyone's hopes, fears or beliefs. His greatness is largely due to this fidelity in a mind of extraordinary power; and if, as a private person, he had a religious faith, his tragic view can hardly have been in contradiction with this faith, but must have been included in it, and supplemented, not abolished, by additional ideas. (Ibid. p. 25)

Green's call to a life of self-sacrifice in the pursuit of the 'higher self', and for the sake of the whole of society, or even of the Spiritual Substance, seems to find brilliantly poignant illustration in the worlds of these plays where our feelings, honestly recorded, are most firmly attached to the man who will lose, who will be defeated, but whose defeat we cannot but think is in the interests of a good greater than himself. We receive (says Bradley)

the impression that the heroic being, though in one sense and outwardly he has failed, is yet in another sense superior to the world in which he appears; is, in some way which we do not seek to define, untouched by the doom that overtakes him; and is rather set free from life than deprived of it. (Ibid., p. 324)

The world of Shakespearean tragedy is then for A. C. Bradley, a world of secular men whose lives yet embody and display the deepest mysteries of our existence. If these plays demonstrate the Hegelian image of a Universe 'animated by a passion for perfection', and crushing the partial perfections of individuals, our inquiry how this is so can be conducted only by investigating the lives of Shakespeare's men and women ('the highest existence in our view'). Hence, of course, Bradley's famous insistence on treating the characters of the plays as if they were real. I accept that this is a critical weakness; it is of course a common weakness in nineteenth-century criticism; and I would only point out that Bradley was as well aware of its dangers as are his critics:

[1] I say substantially; but the concluding remarks on *Hamlet* will modify a little the statements above. [Bradley's note]

To consider separately the action or the characters of a play . . . is legitimate and valuable, so long as we remember what we are doing. But the true critic in speaking of these apart does not really think of them apart; the whole, the poetic experience, of which they are but aspects, is always in his mind; and he is always aiming at a richer, truer, more intense repetition of that experience. (*Oxford Lectures*, pp. 16–17)

The more important point is that his assumption of reality in the characters is a pre-condition of the brilliant kind of inquiry he is conducting. He approaches these crucial instances of the moral life (created with intensity, but without prejudice and without preconceptions) in the same spirit of search as had animated Wordsworth:

> My question eagerly did I renew
> How is it that you live, and what is it you do?

The tragic heroes, like the leech-gatherer, are crucial, for in them the inquirer detects the 'hiding-places of man's power'.

It is particularly the mystery of the evil in the world that seems to be hidden in these brief but brilliant lives:

> Why is it that a man's virtues help to destroy him, and that his weakness or defect is so intertwined with everything that is admirable in him that we can hardly separate them even in imagination? (p. 29)

But, allowing Green's principle that evil comes only from evil, and that good always produces good, it is Bradley's business to prosecute precisely this separation of good and evil. And so he uses his powers to deal with questions of the kind 'How could Iago, so brilliant in intellect, have been so evil?' or 'How could Hamlet, with these gifts, have failed to do what he believed to be the will of Providence?' The action of these plays is a landscape in which the moral lives of the characters are unfolded, and at the centre of their lives lie these questions about the intertwining of good and evil:

What is the answer to that appeal of Othello's:

> Will you, I pray, demand that demi-devil
> Why he hath thus ensnared my soul and body?

This question Why? is *the* question about Iago, just as the question Why did Hamlet delay? is *the* question about Hamlet. (p. 222)

The answer to such central questions must be sought, in Bradley's view, in purely human terms. He rejects the view that Iago loves evil simply because it is evil, because that 'makes him psychologically impossible'. He goes to great pains to reject any sense of demonic possession in *Macbeth*:

> There is no sign whatever in the play that Shakespeare meant the actions of Macbeth to be forced on him by an external power, whether that of the Witches, or of their 'masters', or of Hecate. It is needless therefore to insist that such a conception would be in contradiction with his whole tragic practice.
>
> (Ibid., p. 343)

Macbeth, Bradley is arguing here, is 'perfectly free' to make moral choices, which are, in this respect, exactly the same as the moral choices made by real men in the real world. The lessons we may learn by investigating his case are precisely the lessons that need to be learned for ordinary ethical living. Hence the detail he lavishes on the establishment of the factual reality of the cases; allowances for dramatic vagueness are to be avoided, for they would imply a separation of the play's moral life and that of human beings. The famous series of notes (A–EE)—'Where was Hamlet at the time of his father's death?', 'Did Emilia suspect Iago?', 'When was the murder of Duncan first plotted?'[1] are concerned to close every possible loophole of vagueness. They are more extreme than the body of the text, but they spring from the same central passion that animates the book. Bradley's *Shakespearean Tragedy* could not be the classic work it is if it were not characterized by this tenacity of central viewpoint, accompanied (and critical tenacity

[1] But not, of course, the out-Bradleying Bradley question Leavis proposed to L. C. Knights: 'How many children had Lady Macbeth?'.

is rarely so accompanied) by extreme fair-mindedness in the handling of evidence, and extreme honesty of self-analysis.

The twentieth-century success of Bradley's criticism is very remarkable, if my account of its background is correct. Long after Green's *Prolegomena* is forgotten, long after the Oxford Idealists have been demolished, *Shakespearean Tragedy* goes bowling along, reprint after reprint. Why should this be?

Mrs Warnock has recently remarked of Idealist or Metaphysical ethics that 'The metaphysical pleasure precisely consists in . . . seeing familiar problems, such as the problem of how it is right to behave, somehow reduced, and also answered by being shown to be a part of a total scheme of things. This kind of pleasure may be partially aesthetic; it certainly has very little to do with how many of the propositions contained in the system are actually true statements.'[1]

We may imagine that Green's formulations are especially liable to attacks on their truth of statement. The spiritual power invoked in Green's system was so vague that both Christians and Freethinkers could regard him as of their camp. But this vagueness is a positive necessity in the world invoked by A. C. Bradley. A tragedy which explicitly and precisely invokes supernatural justice is bound to be, to that extent, the less tragic. (The sense of waste in *Dr. Faustus* can only be strong because Marlowe's Christian world is so animated by anti-Christian feeling.) And a tragic world without some sense of spiritual meaning is lamed and deprived, a body without a soul. Shakespeare's tragedies avoid both pitfalls; and what would be vagueness or evasion in a philosophic system is here a recognition that human life is involved in tragic mystery. *Shakespearean Tragedy* is able again and again to suggest the potential of explicit spiritual meaning in the tragic events before us; but is always careful to withdraw before improper definition is required. Thus,

> In *Macbeth* and *Hamlet* not only is the feeling of a supreme power or destiny peculiarly marked, but it has also at times a peculiar tone, which may be called, in a sense, religious. I

[1] *Ethics Since 1900* (1960), p. 47, quoted in Richter, op. cit., p. 190.

cannot make my meaning clear without using language too definite to describe truly the imaginative impression produced; but it is roughly true that, while we do not imagine the supreme power as a divine being who avenges crime, or as a providence which supernaturally interferes, our sense of it is influenced by the fact that Shakespeare uses current religious ideas here much more decidedly than in *Othello* or *King Lear*. (p. 172)

or again,

> ... the result is that the Ghost affects imagination not simply as the apparition of a dead king who desires the accomplishment of *his* purposes, but also as the representative of that hidden ultimate power, the messenger of divine justice set upon the expiation of offences which it appeared impossible for man to discover and avenge, a reminder or a symbol of the connexion of the limited world of ordinary experience with the vaster life of which it is but a partial appearance. And as, at the beginning of the play, we have this intimation, conveyed through the medium of the received religious idea of a soul come from purgatory, so at the end, conveyed through the similar idea of a soul carried by angels to its rest, we have an intimation of the same character, and a reminder that the apparent failure of Hamlet's life is not the ultimate truth concerning him. (p. 174)

This is the closest Bradley ever comes to an explicitly Christian reference in Shakespeare. Usually he prefers the 'in some sense which we do not seek to define' strategy which may be noticed in the quotation from p. 324 given above (p. 112). Later, speaking of feelings evoked by the death of Cordelia, he again moves towards definition.

> It implies that the tragic world, if taken as it is presented, with all its error, guilt, failure, woe and waste, is no final reality, but only a part of reality taken for the whole, and, when so taken, illusive; and that if we could see the whole, and the tragic facts in their true place in it, we should find them, not abolished, of course, but so transmuted that they had ceased to be strictly tragic. (p. 324)

But in a footnote he withdraws from any improper explicitness, any illegitimate extension of the actual experience of the play:

> It follows from the above that, if this idea were made explicit and accompanied our reading of a tragedy throughout, it would confuse or even destroy the tragic impression. So would the constant presence of Christian beliefs. The reader most attached to these beliefs holds them in temporary suspension while he is immersed in a Shakespearean tragedy. Such tragedy assumes that the world, as it is presented, is the truth, though it also provokes feelings which imply that this world is not the whole truth, and therefore not the truth. (p. 325 N.1)

The culpable vagueness of Idealism is no longer culpable here, for it is vague at precisely the point where tragedy *has* to be vague if it is to remain tragic. The system of thought and the work to be analysed are splendidly at one. What the imagination has loved as poetry the critic has enabled us to love as system and as reason.

VII

Edward Thomas, Poet and Critic

R. GEORGE THOMAS

I

EDWARD THOMAS was killed on Easter Monday, 9 April 1917, in the morning during the opening phase of the Battle of Arras. A few days earlier he had received a copy of *The Times Literary Supplement* for the 29 March which contained a review of the first group of his poems to receive critical notice. These eighteen poems by 'Edward Eastaway' were included in *An Annual of New Poetry* along with poems by Gordon Bottomley, W. H. Davies, John Drinkwater, Robert Frost, W. W. Gibson and T. Sturge Moore, and a play by R. C. Trevelyan. The reviewer devoted half of his space to Edward Eastaway whom he found to be a 'real poet, with the truth in him', although, 'like most of his contemporaries, he has too little control over his eyes'. Noting that 'Mr. Eastaway makes his poems wholly out of natural fact' whereas 'Wordsworth passes from it at once to human beings', the reviewer turns aside for a moment to praise Wordsworth's method before asking his own question of the new poetry:

> Is this new method an unconscious survival of a materialism and rationalism which the tremendous life of the last three years has made an absurdity? If spirit is more, much more, than it was three years ago, how can Nature be kept outside the charm of its complete unity? How, above all, can poetry, always the very voice of spirit and prophet of unity, think of Man and Nature except as two aspects of One Life, two children of One Mind?

On April the fourth, in his last letter to his friend Gordon Bottomley, Edward Thomas made his own comment on this review:

I have not seen the Annual yet but by the same post as your letter came the Times review which I was quite pleased with. I don't mind now being called inhuman and being told by a reviewer now that April's here—in England now—that I am blind to the 'tremendous life of these 3 years'. It would be the one consolation in finishing up out here to provide such reviewers with a conundrum, except that I know they would invent an answer if they saw that it was a conundrum. Why do the idiots accuse me of using my eyes? Must I only use them with fieldglasses and must I see only Huns in these beautiful hills eastwards and only hostile flashes in the night skies when I am at the Observation Post?

Recently (in March 1967) his fellow officer, John M. Thorburn, recalled for me this O.P.:

Death came to him instantaneously when alone at the observation post, a scene of pastoral and woodland beauty, strangely, though most appropriately, enshrining the moment of the end. It was there when we happened to be together that he used to try to teach me to see, yet struggle as I might I could never see as he saw. He saw by comprehensive, yet essentially exact, vision of the landscape as, through poetry, he had learned to see, trained as he said of himself in simple direct observation of the country scenes:

In hawthorn time in Wiltshire travelling
In search of something chance could never bring

All had their churches, graveyards, farms and byres
Lurking to one side up the paths and lanes,
Seldom well seen except by aeroplanes.

His was a most signal instance of the manner in which a disciplined poetic gift could be effectually brought up to the harsh demands of the field. Antithetical—one would say—was the gift he had in no small measure, the deliberate but effortless ease with which he could marshal men.

This illuminating triple exchange of opinions forms a suitable introduction to Edward Thomas as poet and critic and, indirectly, it can lead towards some understanding of the man who assumed a pseudonym in order to introduce his most memorable writing to an ever-widening circle of readers. For, in spite of the thirty-eight entries under his name in the British Museum Catalogue—the majority of which are in prose and few of which have ever been reprinted—it is his poems that keep Edward Thomas's name alive. And yet the poetry, like some rediscovered classical torso or, more precisely, like the prominent tip of an iceberg, gains in depth and power when it is read in the light of the fifteen years of continuous writing that preceded its sudden emergence in the autumn of 1914.

II

Undeservedly most of Edward Thomas's prose works have been forgotten: written in response to the unsympathetic demands of publishers and for a public that has long since disappeared, all of his books contain chapters, or sections of chapters, that are irrelevant to their context but vitally necessary to the writer's lifelong desire to communicate his inmost thoughts to the ideal reader. He had begun publishing articles on natural subjects when he was a pupil in the History Eight at Saint Paul's School and his first book, *Woodland Life*, appeared before he went up to Lincoln College, Oxford. His unpublished letters show that in his early years he thought of himself as an essayist but, as he came to depend more and more upon reviewing for a living, he accepted the new limitation imposed upon him and noted, with his usual self-deprecating irony, that the 1,200 word article and the paragraph formed the fixed axis of what he had to say. Constant reviewing was his chief source of income from 1902 until 1910/1911, but he annually undertook to write at least two books each year and, in addition, he worked away at his essays and sketches for his own satisfaction and continued to fill his notebooks with observations of people, things and moods as he followed his lifelong habit of constant travel throughout the south of England and Wales. Eventually, the favourable climate for daily literary journalism created by Massingham and Nevinson changed sharply in favour of more popular values and Edward Thomas was unable to accept the new condition, although editors still retained him as the most acceptable interpreter of new poetry and of country books. In the four years before 1914 he was slowly forced to accept commissions to write four or five books each year at miserable prices; he found, too, that, despite the approval of discriminating judges, his books were inevitably remaindered. At the same time his own health deteriorated and his commercial reputation as a writer suffered.

This four-year period seems to have dominated the memories of those who wrote about him in the first years after his death and formed the staple element of the 'Edward Thomas Legend' that has been current ever since the sarsen stone was erected to his memory by public subscription and ceremony on the Shoulder of Mutton, Steep, in October 1937. Unwittingly, the quotation from his own work inscribed on the Memorial ('And I rose up, and knew that I was tired, and continued my journey') appears to lend a kind of official sanction to the romantic legend that here was a neglected and misunderstood genius, forced to become a hack-writer of unworthy books, who was miraculously transformed by wartime conditions and an accidental meeting with Robert Frost, into a poet. The small grain of truth that lies at the heart of this, as of all legends, provides no justification for any refusal to recognize the underlying unity of all the prose and poetry that Edward Thomas had written for his own satisfaction throughout his adult life. One's understanding of the poetry is severely limited if it is read solely within the context of the *Collected Poems* and without some knowledge of very many passages from his essays and topographical books. It would be an even more restrictive limitation if the poetry were to be read without reference to the poet's thirteen years of critical interpretation of twentieth-century English poetry.

These substantial omissions from our knowledge, which cannot possibly be filled within the terms of this essay, must await the publication of selections from all his prose that would, in the first instance, provide an appropriate context within which the poetry may be read. The value and need of such repair work is clearly demonstrated by two posthumous collections of his prose: *Cloud Castle and Other Papers* (1922), with a brief introduction by W. H. Hudson, and *The Last Sheaf* (1928), with a foreword by Thomas

Seccombe. A quotation from each of these prefaces must stand for
the longer investigation that this subject really demands. Hudson's
unfinished note was the last thing that he wrote: it recaptures a
close friendship with Edward Thomas, born of a working partner-
ship in natural history:

> But there were two or perhaps three things that drew us to-
> gether: first, our feeling for nature, and, secondly, for poetry;
> and as his knowledge of poetic literature was so much pro-
> founder than mine, and his judgement so much more mature, I
> was glad to accept him as my guide in that extensive wilderness.
> I was not always a perfectly docile pupil, as he was intolerant of
> inferior verse, while I took a keen interest in the forgotten
> minor poets of the last century. This was often the subject of
> our conversation, and I had no objection to it. I think, too, or,
> rather, I should say I know it, that the chief reason of the bond
> uniting us was that we were both mystics in some degree. He
> was shy of exhibiting it, and either disguised it or attributed it to
> someone he meets and converses with in his rambles, as in
> 'Cloud Castle', the first sketch in this collection of papers which
> he himself arranged for publication before leaving England. It
> is more manifest in his poetry, that being the medium through
> which a man can best reveal his soul.

Seccombe had walked and cycled with Edward Thomas, and his
foreword was originally a letter to his memory which appeared in
the *Times Literary Supplement* on 16 April 1917. Himself a prolific
writer of books and a scholarly student of George Borrow,
Seccombe was admirably placed to assess Thomas's literary output
with judgement and understanding:

> His knowledge of poetry soon took me out of my depth. To
> the younger men he was a Rhadamanthus and a Cerberus in one.
> He was the man with the keys to the Paradise of English Poetry,
> and probably reviewed more modern verse than any critic of his
> time. The material bulk of it became in the lapse of years a
> source of vexation to him. . . . He acquired the habit of taking
> the books about with him in a heavy valise and leaving them, as
> it were accidentally, at the houses of friends. Of these he had

many, even among poets; and some of them, I know, would regard him as a counsellor unrivalled . . . The quality of his prose was apt to be too costly for the modern market; and the result was often Love and Literature, with its precarious awards, literally in a cottage. His pride in the dignity of letters was intense. The result was much hard work and sometimes unsympathetic collar work mostly of a biographical complexion, the best of which (and in his *Jefferies* and his *Borrow* it is very good indeed) shows marks of fatigue. . . . He was a desperate student of the *genre* that he adopted, and his anthology *This England* is really an artist's notebook. It annotates the life-enthusiasm of a born prosemaster, whose love of this country was as generous as it was instinctive.

Twelve days later Walter de la Mare, in his review of *An Annual of New Poetry* in the *Saturday Westminster Gazette*, paid his own oblique tribute to the influence of Thomas's newspaper criticism on struggling poets:

Edward Thomas must have been a critic of rhymes in his nursery. How much generous help and encouragement many living poets owe to his counsel only themselves could say. To his candour, too. For the true cause, he believed, is better served by an uncompromising 'Trespassers will be prosecuted' than by an amiable 'All are welcome'. Until he became soldier, and so found a fresh and vivid interest, it had been his fate, day in, day out, to write for a living. To a temperament so independent and so self-critical this experience was at times little short of purgatory. . . . For though reading and writing were almost as natural to him as walking and talking, books were for him a fulfilment of life, never a substitute for it; and to those who love him, he meant, beyond most men, a great deal more than his books.

Allowing for the epitaph-like tone of these eulogies composed so close to the poet's death and remembering the fact that all three judgements were made on the strength of a limited knowledge of his total poetic output, they remain, even today, substantially valid comments upon the unity that exists between Edward

I

Thomas's prose and his verse. But they are incomplete guides
both to the slow development of his prose, away from the influence of Pater and in the direction of 'naturalism', and to the
consistency with which he championed those poets of his own
day—now so desperately lumped together under the meaningless
umbrella-term of 'Georgian'—who were trying to bring the
language and rhythm of poetry closer to the natural patterns of
speech. This belief was the indissoluble bond that was forged
between him and Robert Frost: the overt recognition of it by the
American sparked off his own poetry. So that the adoption of
the pseudonym 'Edward Eastaway' was not simply a defence
mechanism against the insincere praise of friends, or the automatic
abuse of hostile critics; it represents, I believe, the poet's clear-
sighted recognition of the culminating change of manner
that had affected his approach to writing once he began to write
verse.

III

This is not a difficult change to chart once the evidence is collected and due allowance is made for the ambivalent attitude he
displayed towards his own ability as a critic of verse. From early
manhood Edward Thomas was tortured by an excess of self-
consciousness which manifested itself, in one way at least, as the
most severe criticism of his own work. But there is no hesitancy
of tone in what he actually wrote. Looking back on his early
development as a writer ('How I Began') he reveals the very
qualities that made him such a firm critic of post-Victorian
verse.

> I ravaged the language (to the best of my ability) at least as much
> for ostentation as for use, though I should not like to have to
> separate the two. This must always happen where a man has
> collected all the colours of the rainbow, 'of earthquake and
> eclipse', on his palette, and has a cottage or a gasometer to paint.
> A continual negotiation was going on between thought, speech
> and writing, thought having as a rule the worst of it. Speech
> was humble and creeping, but wanted too many fine shades and
> could never come to a satisfactory end. Writing was lordly and

regardless. Thought went on in the twilight, and wished the other two might come to terms for ever. But maybe they did not and never will, and, perhaps, they never do.

His approach to criticism was similarly modest and clear-sighted. In October 1902, when he succeeded Lionel Johnson as the literary critic of the *Daily Chronicle*, he outlined his qualifications for the task in a letter to Gordon Bottomley:

> In a week's time I shall be free, I hope, and shall write again. But I will not promise you any criticism. For though I have to live by reviewing, I am most uncritical. I read very much as I eat, and all I know is that a book feeds me or it does not. In my daily work I blame the books that do not feed me, though I have no more right to blame claret because it leaves an unpleasant taste in my mouth. Still, perhaps I know something about technique.

Thirteen years later, a month before he enlisted in the Artists Rifles and seven months after he had begun to write poetry of his own, he apologized to John Freeman for some adverse comments on poems that Freeman had sent to him:

> That is what I am discovering is the ghastly result of reviewing. I have concentrated so much on details and side issues that I really am almost impervious to effects. This is how professional critics must always have gone wrong. They like or think they like one method and not another, and let the principal thing, the effect, go hang, instead of watching first and last for that. I don't mean that great poems do not remind one of one's own experiences but I believe that they are so complete that one does not see the subject apart from the presentation and could not imagine them done otherwise. On the other hand I plead guilty to being quite capable of missing the *effect* by looking, as I said before, at the process of the treatment, as if it were a thing apart, as if I believed (like Monro) that conception and execution were different things. I admit they may seem so but then it may mean either that the writer is unsuccessful or that the reader is not understanding, is captious, or a professional critic like Yours ever, Edward Thomas.

Between the writing of these two letters, he had contributed over a million and a half words of criticism in full-scale reviews to the *Daily Chronicle, World, The Bookman* and the *Morning Post*, apart from his own books and the countless shorter unsigned articles to other journals. It is no surprise, then, that his opinion of the new 'Georgian Poetry' was sought by the editors of the specialized weeklies and monthlies that proliferated between 1910 and 1914. Even before he had met Robert Frost his thinking as a critic was moving towards approval of the kind of poetry that he was himself to write and which, with an irony that he would have readily savoured, has too frequently been lumped together with the products of Harold Monro's Bookshop.

In his reviews of poetry Edward Thomas was incapable of in-sincere praise or meaningless abuse. Trivial versifiers, it is true, were cruelly dismissed. Roden Noel 'wrote verses for three years without knowing that emotion will not flow on to paper like ink'. Of Mr. Swinburne's *A Channel Passage and Other Poems* 'one may say that he has scarcely any material. And yet he plays the same tunes on the same subtle instrument'. He recognizes that

> there is a danger lying in the leaping rhythms that Mr. Alfred Noyes uses so well. Too seldom are the words transmuted into the very things that they describe . . . In *The Golden Hind* this kind of language makes the effect not particular enough, but rather vague and blurred.

Edward Thomas was constantly on the alert for tired worn-out poetic habits that merely echoed the nineteenth-century poets. He finds some of Fiona MacLeod's poems good enough for a place in the 'Celtic Revival',

> but a number seem to have been made to a recipe—the ingre-dients carelessly spread in disorder. These ingredients are the words 'dim', 'sorrow', 'grief', 'old tears', 'the brown leaf'' 'the crying of the wind', etc. Some are mere exercises in sorrow, prompted by the old poetry.

His strong preference for poetry that came closer to the movement of contemporary speech was revealed early, in a review of Yeats's *Deirdre*:

> The piece moves without change of scene, as naturally as any talk, without the intrusion of anything merely poetical, yet with that rich simplicity in which this poet is unequalled. Austerely organic, the play has melody also; it mingles the quality of drama and ballad.

Alone among the popular critics of 1909 Edward Thomas recognized the quality of Ezra Pound's *Personae*:

> Carelessness of sweet sound and of all the old tricks makes Mr. Pound's book rather prickly to handle at first ... We read it for the third time—and it is less than sixty pages—because it was good the second, and, nevertheless, still held back other good things. But we know from experience that it is impossible to show in a bit of a column that a new writer is good in a new way.... For brusque intensity of effect we can hardly compare them with any other work. He is so possessed of his own strong conceptions that he not only cannot think of wrapping them up in a conventional form, but he must ever show his disdain for it a little—one of his poems is, in so many words, a revolt against the crepuscular spirit in modern poetry. When we consider (the volume), there is singularly little crudity, and practically no extravagance. It is mostly hard, naked, and grim.

In *Memories of an Edwardian or Neo-Georgian* Edward Jepson recalls the consternation caused by this favourable review at the Square Club, the literary club of the 'Edwardian Revival' among whose frequent diners were G. K. Chesterton, Walter de la Mare, Algernon Blackwood, John Masefield, John Galsworthy, A. H. Bullen, H. W. Nevinson, Joseph Conrad, Ford Madox Ford and others.

> Poor Edward Thomas! He did look so hot and bothered. His protest that he had acted in good faith, that at the time of the writing of the review he had really fancied that he had liked the

verse of Ezra Pound drew from his colleagues only horrid rumblings. The Club rocked to its foundations and so did English Literature.

Jepson's gossipy memories do not recall that Edward Thomas's judgement of Pound's later works resolutely refused to be rocked: his reviews of Pound continued to show qualified approval until, once more and for the last time, he singled out Pound's contribution to *Des Imagistes: An Anthology* and praised his poems written 'under the restraint imposed by Chinese originals or models'. Jepson recalls no reaction to Edward Thomas's most significant piece of rescue work—the review of Robert Frost's *North of Boston* that appeared in *The New Weekly* on 8 August 1914. This review, which led, first to a rapidly maturing friendship between the two men, and then to Thomas's consequent decision to begin writing poetry, is the culminating point of all that Thomas had thought about lyric poetry during his active life as a reviewer and anthologist. It will best serve as a bridge passage leading to a consideration of his own verse:

I have not met a living poet with a less obvious or more complicated ancestry. Nor is there any brag or challenge about this. Mr. Frost has, in fact, gone back, as Whitman and as Wordsworth went back, through the paraphernalia of poetry into poetry again. With a confidence like genius, he has trusted to his conviction that a man will not easily write better than he speaks when some matter has touched him deeply, and he has turned it over until he has no doubt what it means to him, when he has no purpose to serve beyond expressing it, when he has no audience to be bullied or flattered, when he is free, and speech takes one form and no other. Whatever further discipline was necessary, he has got from the use of the good old English medium of blank verse ... The effect of each poem is one and indivisible. You can hardly pick out a single line more than a single word. There are no show words or lines. The concentration has been upon the whole, not the parts. Decoration has been forgotten, perhaps for lack of the right kind of vanity and obsession ... Naturally, then, when his writing crystallizes, it is often in a terse, plain phrase, such as the proverb, 'Good fences make good neighbours', or 'Pressed into service means pressed out of shape'. But even this kind of characteristic detail is very much less important than the main result, which is a richly homely thing beyond the grasp of any power except poetry. It is a beautiful achievement, and I think a unique one, as perfectly Mr. Frost's own as his vocabulary, the ordinary English speech of a man accustomed to poetry and philosophy, more colloquial and idiomatic than the ordinary man dares to use even in a letter, almost entirely lacking the hackneyed emphatic forms of journalists and other rhetoricians, and possessing a kind of healthy, natural delicacy like Wordsworth's, or at least Shelley's, rather than that of Keats.

It reads, as indeed it is, like an apology for his own life as a writer and points, like a true signpost, to the subsequent development of his own verse.

IV

The poetry of Edward Thomas can appear extremely elusive because it catches so completely the facts of his solitary experiences as a walker and the constant melancholia-inspired debate that frequently dominated his most intimate thoughts and reflections. Among friends, or inside the family circle, he was a delightful singer of all manner of songs and there is abundant testimony to the range and lucidity of his conversation. But there was another equally memorable side to his nature. Frequently his only contribution to long passages of general conversation would be a sharply mordant or salacious phrase—of which only a few have been preserved—and most of his familiar walking companions remember the silent hours of concentrated observation that accompanied his long and effortless stride through little-known and forgotten ways, or across country in response to map and compass. His numerous books and essays bear testimony to a life-long habit of solitary walking that matched his habit of silent, indeed solitary, composition; so that it is no surprise that his poems should be so intensely personal in quality or that the popular anthologists should seize on his nature poems as the most suitable introduction to his poetry for the general reader.

When the war came and most of his paid literary work ceased, Edward Thomas busied himself with two tasks besides a commission to write *The Life and Times of the Duke of Marlborough*: the one he derisively referred to as 'Homes and Haunts of English Authors' (published posthumously in 1917 as *A Literary Pilgrim in England*); the other was the anthology, *This England*, which Thomas Seccombe praised so highly. In no small measure each book bears the marks of the long struggle with himself that finally ended in his enlistment as a soldier and found expression, almost six months later, when he wrote 'This is no case of petty right or wrong' after a long wrangle with his father during his first Christmas leave. Some writers have attributed the growing self-confidence that marked Thomas once he had become a soldier to the orderly pattern of military discipline and the freedom from financial worry that a soldier's pay brought. There *was* a change, but I think it arose from the resolution of this inner debate, the intensity of which is merely hinted at in all the personal correspondence that remains.

Among so much conjecture one fact is of great significance: Robert Frost, who seems to have been most privy to Edward Thomas's thinking during the summer and autumn of 1914, eventually failed to convince his friend to return with him to New Hampshire in February 1915. This is not surprising. His ties with the England of 1915 were nurtured by a profound sense of continuity with the past which had found expression time and again in his essays and reviews. His comments on W. H. Hudson ('What he reverences and loves is the earth, and the earth he knows is, humanly speaking, everlasting') and Richard Jefferies ('In his home-country we are in a spirit-land') can be matched against a startling paragraph which he once tacked on to the end of a *Daily Chronicle* book review in 1908:

But because we are imperfectly versed in history, we are not therefore blind to the past. The eye that sees the things of today, and the ear that hears, the mind that contemplates or dreams, is itself an instrument of antiquity equal to whatever it is called upon to apprehend. We are not merely twentieth-century

Londoners or Kentishmen or Welshmen. We belong to the past with Taliesin, Alexander, Noah. And of these many folds in our nature the face of the earth reminds us, and perhaps even where there are no more marks visible upon the land than there were in Eden, we are aware of the passing of time in ways too difficult and strange for the explanation of historian or zoologist. It is this manifold nature that responds with such indescribable depths and variety to the appeal of many landscapes.

Undoubtedly, then, although the 'nature poems' provide a legitimate point of entry into the world of this poet, so endowed with extraordinary powers of observation, this is no simple pictorial world: time as well as space provides its axis of reference.

The poems were written rapidly, almost tumultuously: the 141 poems in *Collected Poems* was composed between late November 1914 and December 1916, and for two-thirds of that time he was a soldier in various camps in the south of England. As far as one can judge from the extant notebooks and scattered manuscripts and typescripts, after an initially faltering start—in the course of which a few early poems were much altered and reshaped—most of his poetry was written as smoothly as he had written his reviews and books, easily and with little significant alteration except at the proof-stage. His letters show quite unmistakably that, during his years as a 'prose-master', he followed the same working method. First, he laboured long and hard at his material, taking endless pains to be accurate and thorough; but once he had settled down to write, his pen moved effortlessly over the page until exhaustion, or fatigue, or disgust, caused him to stop. The composition of his poems seems to have followed the same compulsive pattern and his own term for the early stages of his verse-writing was that 'it had begun to run'. Writing verse took the place of the personal essay writing that he had practised since his undergraduate days and that he had collected, at regular intervals, in volumes like *Light and Twilight*, *Rose Acre Papers* and *Rest and Unrest*. Significantly enough, these essays were almost always the result of the periods he spent at home between the interminable rambles in search of copy, or the ceaseless hunt for books in the British

Museum, that had characterized his preparation for *Wales, Oxford, The Icknield Way, George Borrow, Richard Jefferies* or *The Feminine Influence on the Poets.* Most of his poems were written either at Steep (or his parents' home in Balham) or in various army camps (at Handel Street, Gidea Park and Trowbridge). A handful of them reflect immediate impressions of visits to friends or members of his family, but none are directly about the military life of the camps in which, as his letters show, he was so irresistibly absorbed. Like his essays and narrative sketches, his poetry draws, with remarkable fidelity, upon incidents, moods and experiences that he had sought to express throughout his writing life. In the strictest sense, his poetry is not so much an *apologia* as a *summa* of the inner life of Edward Thomas and for this purpose the *persona* of 'Edward Eastaway' was a necessary creation.

The order in which his verse is printed in *Collected Poems* (Faber and Faber) is a random one and, despite the admirable bibliographical note in that standard volume, it gives no indication of the exact development of the poetry. In particular, there is no indication that the volume entitled *Last Poems* (1918) consists of poems that were chiefly composed before the sixty poems that preceded them in *Poems* (1917). When read in order of composition the poems seem to follow a clearly emerging pattern that leads away from pure description—based on the 'prose-poems' that Robert Frost had insisted were present in a volume like *In Pursuit of Spring*—and towards the later poems of introspective self-analysis which, to many critics, have constituted the elusive element in Edward Thomas's poetry. For it has never been easy to 'place' his poetry either among the Georgian writers or among the War Poets: his poetry has little of the directness and simplicity of 'Georgian' verse—whatever that term may mean. Edward Thomas wrote many poems about life in rural surroundings but these 'nature' poems do not form the bulk of his poetry and more than direct descriptions of places or scenes can be said to dominate those of his books which are loosely described as 'topography'. Certainly, *The Icknield Way, In Pursuit of Spring* and *The South Country* were written by a countryman with an intimate knowledge of the districts he describes, but the true subject of all three books is the author himself and the people he met on his travels, or, more exactly one suspects, the people he imagined as he walked. For few English writers since Chaucer have so peopled their account of a journey with imaginary folk that yet carry about them the ostensible marks of realistic pursuits. His poems draw naturally and inevitably upon a lifelong observation of natural objects and they are as full of sharply edged geological features as they are of trees and birds and flowers, accurately, but not obtrusively, perceived and set down. This side of Edward Thomas's poetry needs no elaboration here; but perhaps it will be worth while to consider some of the human beings (or voices) who speak through his poems.

His poems, like his prose books, abound with records of itinerant encounters. Himself a welcome member of some of London's most celebrated luncheon gatherings, where good talk was even more important than food and drink, he yet chose to spend long intervals of his life in a solitude that was often shared with imaginary conversationalists; for, in all his writing between 1902 and 1916, the records of his acute observation were never complete until they had been tested against the protagonists of an internal debate. True to his theory that post-Victorian verse should renew itself from the language of spoken usage, the *dramatis personae* of these wayside duologues are ordinary people who seem to grow out of the landscape they typify, and then to fade back into it. This poet, who was 'himself denied any natural respect of ceremonial use', believed that

> some men, particularly sailors and field labourers, but also navvies and others who work heavily with their hands, have this glory of use. Their faces, their clothes, their natures, all appear to act and speak harmoniously, so that they cause a strong impression of personality which is to be deeply enjoyed in a world of masks, especially of black clerical masks.

(Five years later, in his little book on *The Country*, he developed the point even more explicitly with his usual quiet irony:

When a poet writes, I believe he is often only putting into

words what such another old man puzzled out among the sheep in a long lifetime. You cannot persuade me that the peakfaced poets think of all those things about earth and men by themselves.)

In someone else such pronouncements could be construed as the essences of 'Georgianism': an embodiment of the Londoner's weekend escape into Surrey, away from the smoke in search of the first cuckoo and the inspiration required for a 'poem'. Edward Thomas was no Cockney escapist. He had built his frugal way of life upon his faith in the healing power to be gained from a life lived in close contact with country things and, among the Southern English equivalents of Wordsworth's Dalesmen who talk through his poems, he himself is the most constant interlocutor.

His poems contain the archaeology (it is not too loose a term) of his own multi-layered personality. Becoming a soldier allowed him to share in 'the glory of use' in a manner satisfying to his intellectual and moral nature: it also gave him some relief from the nagging search for his own identity that was part of his acute melancholia. Anchored in routine and relieved of all immediate ends except that of self-expression in his leisure moments, he pursued tirelessly in his verse the sources of his own past happiness and sorrow and, in the course of this quest, sought to recapture his frequently recorded consciousness of identity with all living things, past and present. For him a calm sea had been

incomparable except to moods of the mind. It is then as remote from the earth and earthly things as the sky, and the remoteness is the more astonishing because it is almost within our grasp.

Equally central to his way of thinking was the weight of the past: 'There are enough of the dead; they outnumber the living.'

Following such clues from his most personal prose, we can more easily interpret the apparent elusiveness of so much of his best verse and sharpen the focus of our attention when reading poems like 'There was a time', 'Roads', 'The Chalk-Pit', 'Beauty', 'The Wind's Song', 'Wind and Mist', 'The Brook' and 'Aspens'.